ENDOR

"When it comes to looking up when problems pull you down, my dear friend Care Tuk wins the award. She may have more nuts, bolts, screws, and hinges in her body than the house in which I live, so when Care speaks about triumphs through pain and suffering, I listen! Her new collection of insights will uplift and inspire, so consider the book you hold in your hands a treasure!"

Joni Eareckson Tada

Joni and Friends International Disability Center

"While I've met hundreds of thousands of cancer patients over the last 25 years, as a two-time survivor myself, I don't believe I will ever come across someone more resilient than Care Tuk. Always positive, never discouraged, and most certainly full of humor, her attitude is contagious no matter what life throws your way. So grab a copy of Don't Wimp Out and get prepared to turn your life around."

Christine Clifford

CSP; CEO/President of the Cancer Club
Author of Not Now...I'm Having a No Hair Day!
and nine other books about cancer

"You'll laugh, you'll cry, you'll journey with Care as though you were sitting with a mug of hot cocoa in her Alaskan living room by the fire as she encourages your heart to press on through the battles of life...and you will believe you can as you hear how she has, through seemingly unsurmountable obstacles with hilarity, joy and transparency."

Kristen Morrow Ara

Southwestern Divisional CoordinatorYoung Life/ Capernaum Ministry

"You will be transformed as you experience Care's grit, grace, and faith as you read Don't Wimp Out! Through her words and her example, she leaves indelible heart prints as her servant's heart encourages you with her words of wisdom and discernment and Godly life."

Electra Ariail

My Gratitude Buddy.com and OWN Ambassador

"Care Tuk is the bionic woman of the twenty-first century. Her perseverance through her journey is simply outstanding and inspiring. In Loose Screws and Skinned Knees we learned the background of Care's medical journey that shaped her life. In Don't Wimp Out, you will see her raw humor and incredible faith that has sustained her and her family through the most trying of times. Be prepared to weep, laugh, and shake your head in amazement when you read this dynamic book."

Kelly Marre LMSW

Author of Killing Leuk

"Everyone needs to know how to get through tough times. After reading Don't Wimp Out! you will want to read it over and over to remind you how to get through your moments of wimpy-ness."

David Naster

You Just Have to Laugh - Comedian, Speaker, Filmmaker and Author

"Seems simple. Isn't easy. Care Tuk's words are simple, her life isn't easy. Her stories and messages range from sweet to shocking, from thought provoking to inspiring. Her resilience, faith, and remarkable marriage can take readers to complex territories of disbelief and miracles."

Linda Hawes Clever, MD MACP

Founding President of RENEW

author of The Fatigue Prescription, Four Steps to Renewing Your Energy, Health and Life and the former Editor of the Western Journal of Medicine.

"Care Tuk is a warrior extraordinaire with a sense of humor that just won't stop. She has a way of telling a story that will keep you smiling throughout the day as you recall some bit of it to mind. More important, she isn't afraid to stand firm for the Lord and in Him. As a writer, she shares her good times and bad, but always that thread of her faith is there to encourage. With all she's been through she gives the phrase, "the Lord isn't through with you yet" new meaning. I'm privileged to call her friend and to recommend you pick up one of her books and a cup of something warm to drink, and enjoy the ride."

Tracie Peterson

USA-Today best-selling and award-winning author of over one hundred books

FINDING FAITH, COURAGE and
VICTORY in LIFE'S DAILY BATTLES

DON'T WIMP OUT!

CARE TUK

Don't Wimp Out!
By Care Tuk

Cover and book design : Don Woodward / Ideawave / www.ideawave.com
Editing : Inkwell/Kimberley Woodhouse and Peterson Ink, Inc. / Tracie Peterson

Unless otherwise indicated, Scripture quotations are taken from *The Life Application Bible®, New International Version® Copyright1988, 1989, 1990, 1991* Published jointly by *Zondervan Publishing House* and *Tyndale House.* All rights reserved worldwide.

ISBN: 978-1-7374514–0-2
Printed and published in the United States of America
A/T Printing and Publishing – Anchorage, Alaska

This book is dedicated to

my "toe-mater-sandwich-makers":

You are forever contagious joy.

Your big, bright eyes, so full of wonder—

fill my heart with "this much" love and s'mores!

You never cease to amaze me.

I am truly blessed!

TABLE OF CONTENTS

Endorsements 1

Preface 13

From the Author 15

1. And Yet Another Day 19

2. Blindsided 23

3. Why (K)not? 29

4. Lesson of the Ring 33

5. Promises Kept 37

6. No One Told Us About This Part 41

7. I Didn't Know Catrating a Bull Was Part of My "I Do's" 47

8. Gathering Wisdom 53

9. Doubt 57

10. From Dreams To Dread and Dismay to Delight 61

11. Delinquents 69

12. Debt is a Four Letter Word 73

13. From Beauty and Ashes and Back Again 77

14. Breaker, Breaker – You Got a Copy? 81

15. Round Two 85

16. When the Ash Settled 89

17. Our Summer Surprise 95

18. Humility and the House-Husband 99

19. Double Debt 103

20. Flipped Out Over a Fixer-Upper 107

21. Jesus With Skin On 113

22. Crash and Burn Brightly 117

23. Mom and Dad to Many 123

24. Generational Love 129

25. Battle Ready 133

26. You've Been Served 137

27. Water, Water Everywhere - Lower 48 Style 143

28. Splish-Splash 147

29. Super Troopers 153

30. Toolbox Tips 157

31. All for One and One for All 161
32. I Need a Break 165
33. I Wish Time Was Extinct...171
34. In the Pits 177
35. Hearing vs. Listening.. 181
36. Cast in Concrete.. 185
37. Moving and More 189
38. Casting Out Our Net of Faith 193
39. When Unexpected Becomes Real 197
40. What In the World Just Happened? 201
41. Moving Miracles 207
42. Forever Friends 211
43. The Girls 215
44. Hammering Away...219
45. Great Expectations 223
46. Computers and Chicken Feet.. 227
47. Dreams Do Come True 231
48. So What Does Disability Look Like.................................... 235
49. Wheelchairs are NOT for Wimps 239
50. Seasons Change and So Do Lives 249
51. Failure Is Not an Option... 255
52. You Live In a What?... 259
53. Remember Your Song 263
54. Have You Taken Your Vitamin B3 Today........................... 267
55. Water, Water Everywhere – Alaska Style 271
56. Come Out, Come Out, Wherever You Are 277
57. I'm in Energy Conservation Mode.................................... 281
58. Spoiler Alert: There Is No "Normal" in Alaska.................. 283
59. On the Grounds Of Grief 287
60. Celebrating Life 293
61. Does Job Have Sister?... 297
62. One Last Story 303
Resources... 313
About the Author 319

PREFACE

You've been there. You've done that. You even have the t-shirt. The t-shirt looks worn out, tattered around the edges, and full of holes. Just like you often feel.

Expired past its usefulness, the worn, shabby shirt gets thrown into the rag drawer until a new use for it can be found. You may find yourself in the same place: unused, feeling beaten down. Maybe you have been relegated to the unemployment line or are looking for a new job, desperately wanting to be found valuable again.

Perhaps you find yourself at the end of your proverbial, frayed rope—sweating bullets, frantically hanging on for dear life. You might feel like a failure. At your wit's end, you wonder what will happen if you let go.

Debt may have a stronghold on you—affecting every part of your life including those around you.

Maybe you feel yourself suffocating, about to buckle under the heavy load of uncertainty that dawns with each new day.

In one fell swoop, solid, life-long relationships abruptly change. And not for the better.

Possible tragedy, illness, or an accident—all out of your control—slams you broadside. Feeling like you have been swept up in a tornado, you mumble under your breath, "Toto, we are *not* in Kansas anymore."

Wild fires and thundering storms rage within your soul.

Torrential downpours, flood swelling rain, and hurricane force winds leave damage untold around you. The earth trembles and quakes. A mountain erupts before your very eyes.

How can this be?

Time has flown. Sometimes you feel decades older than your legitimate age because of life's ups and downs, while at others, you wonder how the years have passed in such a blur and what you missed in the meantime. Unfortunately, the calendar hanging on the wall doesn't lie.

Now you're at a place where you've begun to feel inept in a world that is ever-changing. Measured not in inches or feet, but in gigs, bytes, streaming ability, and how fast your internet is.

Technology exponentially races at an unprecedented pace, making you feel like a dinosaur.

We long for the day we go to the mailbox and find a real life *handwritten* note. We hope for connection via a phone call or in-person get-together rather than just a text, social media message, or email.

You drop to your knees. You plead with God—the One and only true God. He is the God who listens, the Great Physician, the Almighty Comforter, The Light, the Great I AM. He is the One who holds the answers to the deepest cries of your heart.

You pray, longing to hear His voice. You feel like the lights of Heaven are on, but No One is home. Or maybe He's just not listening to *you*.

Sound familiar?

If so, *Don't Wimp Out!*

All is *not* lost. There *IS* hope.

It comes one day, one hour, sometimes one minute at a time, and never too late—'cuz God is in the details, *all* the time.

FROM THE AUTHOR

I thought it might be helpful for those who haven't read my first book, *Loose Screws and Skinned Knees*, to have a chance to get to know me a little bit. For those who *have* read the book and have been asking for more, thanks for being patient.

Hi, my name is Care. Just like: care package, Care Bear™, or who cares? I've heard, "Take Care!" often enough my standard answer is, "I have to. I can't get rid of her." If I am with Bill—my husband—he replies, "I have to. I'm married to her."

For inquiring minds, our last name—Tuk—is Dutch. On occasion, people have added a "c" to the spelling. But no, it's not something you do to your shirttails, an item in the pharmaceutical aisle, or a Tuk-tuk taxi in Thailand. And sadly, we have no relation to the famous Friar in *Robin Hood*.

I tell my story in *Loose Screws and Skinned Knees*. And not to rehash it here, but to give you a tiny glimpse, I need to explain a few things.

I am a fourteen—yes, *fourteen*—time cancer survivor. My mother took the drug DES (Diethylstilbestrol a drug used in the 1940's and 1950's meant to prevent miscarriages), when she was pregnant with me. While this drug prevented my mother's body from snuffing out my life, there were many side effects whose impact not known at the time, have plagued me for years to come. Immune deficiencies, fibromyalgia, degenerative joint disease, female cancers, infertility, and hormone issues, are all side effects—now well-documented.

I had my first of many knee surgeries when I was sixteen, and one short month after my mom died from colon cancer. The very same kind of cancer I've survived for over ten years. And it's not the only one I can claim as a survivor. I've been fighting various cancers since I was nineteen-years old. Over four decades.

While cancer has been one of my toughest battle opponents, so was being hit by a drunk driver in 1985. The car accident happened three short days after we had received a letter stating our application to be long-term foreign missionaries had been approved. Our elation of three days prior swiftly turned to devastation. We knew with my significant injuries rehab might take many months, possibly years and best addressed in the United States vs. being on foreign soil.

In our disappointment, we've held onto the valuable truth my wise husband shared: "Our *call* to the mission field has not changed—just the *place*. Our sphere of influence is always and only as far away as the end of our hand. Not just at church, but in our everyday lives – whether we are at the grocery store, at school, in the hospital, at doctor appointments, or even on a construction site. Wherever we are, at any given moment that is where our calling/assignment is."

We cling to this truth and remind each other of it often. We choose to go onward and upward. No regrets.

Another life altering battle occurred following a rare, three compartment subdural brain bleed in late August 2001. My head was bolted and screwed back together. My speech, walking, and daily functioning were severely impacted. When I began to speak again—and still today when I'm tired or over-stimulated—my words came out how Yoda™ speaks. I speak in subject- object-verb syntax.

I still have about thirty words that never came back. Words like alphabet and salmon come out as 'ablaphet" and "slamon." (Try living in Alaska and not able to say *that* fish's name!) Additionally, words with more than two syllables often trip me up.

But, you know what? I'm honored others compare me to the *Star Wars™* hero. After all, he is *kinda* cute! Yoda™ is filled with wisdom and discernment. He is able to discern the light and dark side of a person. Yoda™ speaks very much from his heart, and is a consummate encourager. I love to quote one of Yoda's ™ famous phrase: "Do. Or do not. There is no try."

Yoda™ is a leader, a teacher, yet ever humble. He doesn't seek the limelight. He is firm when counseling younger Jedi Warriors™ training them to let go of everything they fear.

While the above qualities are ones I hope others see in me, our speech makes the two of us—Yoda™ and me—true kindred spirits. For we know (in Yoda™ speak): "K-O-Be" we will *always* be -because the *True* Force is with us. And His name is God.

Walking through the many challenges I have faced (and am still facing); I am a firm believer you can either be *in* pain or *be* a pain. I choose the first. To be honest, I'm never *out* of pain. I'd love to *feel* better, or *be* normal, but I'm not sure I'd recognize either! Hopefully as you read further, you will see I truly have no regrets for the many challenges and adversity we've encountered.

The same can be true for you. Life is difficult for everyone. There are speed bumps and accidents and disasters waiting around almost every corner. That's the point. I know you might be going through some horrendous issues of your own right now. And I want this book to encourage you to not give up.

I pray my goal of sharing hope, humor, and encouragement is met.

I pray your courage will be found as you remember to pace, prioritize, and know your limitations. I also pray you will discover and realize as you keep faith, family, and *fun* as tenets, your battles *can* and *will* be won—especially when you put your trust in and cling to the One above. He never fails.

Never.

1

AND YET ANOTHER DAY

The shrill sound of the telephone jolted me from a deep sleep. I groaned, "It's still 0-dark thirty," to no one in particular.

Okay, so it was only 5:30 a.m., but *I* certainly was not up at the ungodly, still-dark-because-it-was-fall-in-Alaska hour. The last thing I remembered through the cobwebs of slumber before the ringing interruption was my husband, Bill, praying over me. He'd asked God to give me rest and strength for the day, as well as safety for him as he drove the two-hour commute to his job. He untangled the covers, tenderly kissed me, and finished with his usual, "Love you, Lady."

Bill has prayed over me, every single day, for over 45 years. It's a beautiful thing.

As chief inspector for an engineering consulting firm, adventures led him to various parts of Alaska. His commutes to a job were far from boring. One day he might drive a snow-machine, (the Alaskan word for a snowmobile) or another day, a four-wheeler. When working on a remote Native village job site, a dog sled might be his transportation. Then there are *other* times—when his patience is tested. Those are the days when he's in stop-and-go traffic on the highway on his way to job sites in South Central Alaska metro areas.

On this particular morning, after he prayed for me, he'd left for a job in Talkeetna. He always had to make sure he had enough time to account for the unpredictable driving weather in late-fall Alaska. It wasn't unusual to encounter fog, ice, or early snow. As Alaskans know, the possibility of a moose popping out of nowhere, awkwardly ambling across the highway could happen at any moment!

The phone at the house rang. My thoughts went back to the same thing. *Who could be calling at this hour?*

I clumsily groped around the nightstand, knocking the portable phone handset off its stand. "Great," I mumbled to myself. The phone had rolled under the bed. Half-leaning off of the bed, I felt the blood rush to my head as my hands groped around under the bed. Finally, I grabbed the handset.

Squinting, I attempted to make out the number on the caller ID. Without my glasses, I was blind as a bat. Blurry as it was, I recognized the number. Icy fear grabbed me. It was Bill's work phone number.

He never called me from work… not unless there was something wrong. My heart felt like it had jumped into my throat. I could hardly swallow. My imagination ran wild. The roads *had* been getting icy lately. My greatest daily prayer for Bill was his safety making to and from work.

Awkwardly, my fumbling fingers finally found the talk button.

"Hello?" I managed to croak out, trying not to sound as terrified as I felt.

"Quick! Get a pen and paper." Bill bellowed.

Finding my worried wife voice, I rapidly fired questions at him, as if shooting bullets from a semi-automatic rifle. "Are you okay?" "Were you in an accident?" "Did you hit a moose?"

"Settle down, woman. I'm fine." I could hear a chuckle in his voice.

As I wildly scrambled and searched for a scrap of paper, Bill blurted out, "I know the introduction for the next book."

Bill had the intro for the *next* book? The first book, *Loose Screws and Skinned Knees* hadn't made its way back from the printing company in the Lower 48 to our house in Alaska yet. I was totally befuddled.

So let's stop for a minute and get a few things out there. I am married to a man who rarely reads unless absolutely necessary. He rarely writes unless *unquestionably* necessary.

Bill is a burly, steel-wool teddy bear, former ninth in the nation heavy-weight wrestler, who has vocal pipes making heads turn when he blasts out worship songs. He is a construction worker extraordinaire. Constantly in demand, he is a rare breed who can figure out complex situations and fix them with baling wire.

And he called me to tell me *he* had something he wanted *me* to write down?

Bill said, "I know, this may sound bizarre, but write this down. I'll explain when I get home."

After dinner, my husband explained what he wanted me to write down. He told me he had turned off pulled-off to a viewpoint overlooking the Talkeetna Valley. Denali, (aka and formerly known as Mt. McKinley) was out in all of its 'Great One' glory. Two eagles soared on thermals in the foreground. Watching in awe, Bill felt like God whispered to him:

"A time to reflect,
A time to pray;
But most of all,
A time to thank God
For Yet Another Day."

"Got it, Lady?" If you haven't noticed yet, Lady is Bill's nickname for me. *And Yet Another Day* could introduce the chapters and stories to encourage others not to wimp out!"

I couldn't believe my ears. God had given my husband a *poem?* I'm not about to argue with God, much less my husband! I *had* to believe my heart. It was bursting bigger than the Grinch ever dreamed of, even at 0-dark-thirty!

Fast forward six months. I was sitting in my recliner preparing for an upcoming speaking engagement. The first book, *Loose Screws and Skinned Knees*, had arrived. I picked up my sticky-note-filled copy of the book. I wanted to review a few "Alaskan gold nuggets" I planned to share.

Imagine my complete and utter astonishment when my eyes settled on the second to last paragraph of the last chapter. I looked out the window. Goose bumps ran up my arms as The Big One, our eagle introduced in Book One, soared overhead.

I read the paragraph again. Bill and I don't use phrases like *"and yet another day"* in our everyday conversation. But there it was on page 166: "Yet another day for adventuring—even through adversities and obstacles." *And Yet Another Day*. It was our *God*-incidence, our affirmation. Yes, eventually I'd write another book.

And here it is.

I hope as you join me for more stories of adventures and opportunities, you *Don't Wimp Out*. Remember each challenge, each battle, each opportunity and adventure, lay waiting for *your* sphere of influence—right at the end of your hand. Faith, courage and victory in life's daily battles will be found.

2

BLINDSIDED

January 1975. It was a typical, Pacific Northwest Saturday afternoon. I was in my junior year of college. A cold, misty rain accompanied me as I made my way to the University's gymnasium, three blocks from the college-owned house where I lived. Let's get clear on one very important point: I was only going to the gymnasium because I *had* to.

For the single-class Winter Term, I signed up for what sounded like an "easy" course. My brain needed a break from pre-med/OT science courses. Deliberating on what to take, I came upon a class titled, *Sports Appreciation*. In high school, I had been a competitive swimmer, basketball and volleyball player, plus an avid skier. Add those to my love of the outdoors and the fact the course completed my physical education requirement I needed for graduation—and the class equaled perfection.

One mandatory class assignment was to watch a collegiate wrestling match. I had *zero* interest in a sport where two men proved their strength and prowess by contorting their bodies on a sweaty gym mat. Ugh! I thought it was a *disgusting* sport. But like it or not the decision was not mine to make. I'd have to watch the event and learn the rules and rigors of this so called "sport."

When I arrived at the gym, I surveyed the crowd. I positioned myself at the very end of the gym bleachers, closest to the exit door. Instead of sitting on the hard, cold, metal bleacher bench, I leaned up against the solid back edge of the bleachers—you know, just so I could make a quick get-away as soon as the mandatory assignment was complete. There was no way I wanted to be exposed to the sweaty aroma of wrestlers and their mats any longer than I had to.

Little did I realize I stood inches from where the competing wrestlers entered the gym prior to their designated weight-class match.

WHAP!!

Something bumped me, making me lose my balance. It literally made my head spin. And in the moment, I wasn't sure what hit me.

When I pulled my senses together, I looked up. *It* was a *he*. And *he* had drop-dead gorgeous brown eyes.

I pulled in a tiny breath as recognition hit. Wow. This guy... he was one of the University's star athletes in football and wrestling. I also thought I recognized him as one of the students in the Sports Appreciation class I was taking.

He shot a shy, coy, little boyish smile my way—almost like he was trying to apologize for bumping into me—as he made his way to his appointed match.

I turned around. This mammoth of a man *couldn't* have smiled at *me*. He must have smiled at the gorgeous, blonde-haired beauty with curves in all the right places sitting in the bleachers next to where I was standing.

Me? I had a short pixie-like hair style. I had an athletic build, with curves in all the *wrong* places—or no curves at all! I was a wall-flower, who had never really dated. Remember, I was only in the college gym because it was a *mandatory* Winter Term class assignment—to watch a wrestling match I could care less about.

As the heavy-weight class match progressed, the local athlete who'd shot a smile in my direction, picked up his 350 pound opponent in a backward bear hug and lifted the behemoth wrestler up in the air. I heard a voice in the crowd yell, "So, what are you going to do with him now, clown?" (For your amusement, I should share I came to know some time later it was his father calling him out.)

The match ended. The local Mr. Incredible won. As people filed out of the gymnasium, cheerleaders from the visiting team were talking amongst themselves.

"Did you *see* their hulk in the heavy-weight match?"

"He picked our guy totally off the ground!"

"I wonder what they feed him."

A voice from a squat, five-foot-tall woman interrupted their conversation, "Raw meat. Three times a day—whether he wants it or not!"

Everyone chuckled.

The proud and sassy woman was none other than the wrestler's mother.

Never in a million years could I know this big, burly, 9th in the nation heavy-weight wrestler had any remote chance of becoming the man of my wildest dreams – my hope beyond hope, my husband—the one whom God had chosen to be my best friend, spiritual head, and side-kick.

Blindsided.

And not just at the match. You see, a week later, I was in desperate need to pass the Winter Term final exam. I could no more understand wrestling rules than would be on the exam than I could a chemical periodic table. I commiserated my dilemma to a dear childhood friend I ran into on the way to class. She lived on the sorority/fraternity side of campus, so we rarely saw each other. She shared she was friends with one of the wrestlers on our college team. I had no clue that the two of them had seriously dated, prior to her meeting her true soul-mate and now husband.

"In fact," she stated, "I might be able to get him to help you understand the wrestling rules, *plus* he could give you a ride to my wedding. You can't drive, being in a foot to ankle cast and I so I want him at the wedding. I know it's hard for him – he told me not to expect to see him. We ended our conversation with her agreeing to stop by our house, after class, when my housemate, also a mutual high school friend, would be home, to run the idea by her.

Later, the three of us gathered in the kitchen, chit-chatting away. The subject of the possible study date came up; my two friends looked at each other. Apparently my housemate knew this wrestler, too. With glee in their eyes, smirks on their faces and mischievous twinkles in their eyes, they agreed this athlete would be perfect answer to the predicaments for studying *and* a ride to the wedding.

If I wasn't so desperate to pass the exam, a team of wild horses couldn't get me to agree to this arrangement.

Begrudgingly, I let them arrange the study-date for the next day.

If I didn't admit to being hesitant, I'd be lying. I sorely needed help to pass the exam. The grade on it could make or break my chances of getting into The School of Occupational Therapy. I needed a high score.

Sunday afternoon arrived.

The thunderous knock at the front door announced the arrival of my study date. It sounded more like a SWAT team trying to crash the door down. Tentatively, and ever so slowly I opened the door.

Holy-moley! It was the raw-meat-eating, 'clown' from the wrestling match! I slammed the door in horror as I glared at my house-mate.

Blindsided.

"No! Not *him*!" I hissed at my house-mate who was peeking through her bedroom door, her giggles barely muffled by her hand. She was grossly unsuccessful at her attempt to stifle her delight.

Closing my eyes, I shook my head. They had set me up with *the* BMOC (Big Man on Campus—literally *and* figuratively.) He was the football and wrestling hero, a frat-boy, and he was oh, *so* easy on the eyes! My stomach churned.

Sheepishly, I re-opened the door and apologized for my impolite reaction.

We made our way to the kitchen, where I offered him some refreshments. He sat down at the kitchen table and was quick to accept the offer. He chugged down several sodas and ate almost a dozen homemade, chocolate-chip cookies before we got to the task at hand.

As the study-date wore on, the clock ticked away. He repeated, then repeated a second time, and patiently repeated for a *third* time—the basic rules and regulations of college wrestling. While he laboriously repeated the rules, I found myself *un*-laboriously staring deep into his dark, chocolate-brown eyes and admiring his rippling muscles.

Even though I noticed he stared back at me, I simply thought he was attentive and furtive in his duty to help me pass the Winter Term exam.

Several hours passed. We eventually gave up studying. It was to no avail. He had done his best to help me understand the rules and regulations of wrestling. But it was still Greek to me. The conversation changed to general chit-chat. Minutes turned into hours. Before we knew it, the early rays of sunlight peek through the kitchen windows, announcing a new day.

Sometimes being blindsided isn't so bad. Blind faith can be the best kind of faith to have—no expectations, no high hopes, or pitfalls. Maybe this won't be so bad after all.

Then again…

3

WHY (K)NOT?

Bill gave me a ride to the wedding a few weeks later – a gesture of kindness felt by not just me, but my friend he had seriously dated. We left shortly after the reception, once my punch, coffee and tea serving obligation was met. It was late afternoon.

On a whim, Bill suggested we grab a bite to eat, since neither of us had eaten since breakfast. We settled on a nearby restaurant famous for its pasta dishes. I'm not sure if it was the punch we had partaken of, or Cupid's arrow—but neither of us finished even a quarter of our meal. When our waiter came over asking if we were done for the umpteenth time, we self- consciously said yes, not realizing how much time (almost 2 hours) had passed, and how badly the busy restaurant needed our table.

Neither Bill nor I were ready to return to our campus digs. Instead, we drove around in his 1967 MGB convertible, top down, and the wind flying through our hair. (Yes, we *both* sported hair in those days!) We drove around for hours, talking and laughing the entire time, getting to know more about each other. We discovered we both had a strong faith in God and a passion for foreign missions. We discovered we each had suffered the loss of a family member – he, a sister when he was thirteen years old, and me, my mother when I was sixteen. We talked about if each other eventually wanted kids and the myriad of adventures life could hold.

I was flabbergasted. I had totally misjudged this frat-boy jock.

As midnight approached, we found ourselves close to campus. Passing the local movie theater, we saw the marquee announced a midnight debut showing of a new Walt Disney™ movie. Bill mischievously looked at me and asked, "Wanna go?"

Not to be outdone, I playfully answered, "Why not?!"

We couldn't believe we were the *only* ones in the theater.

After the movie, we left the empty theater in the wee hours of the next day. Bill informed me the former day's activities couldn't be considered a "real" date, since it started out as a ride to a wedding.

He suggested our first *real* date could be the following night, if I agreed to accept his invitation. While it was easy to say yes to the date, I learned I should have asked him *specifically* what he had planned. The movie *Blazing Saddles*™ was not on *my* radar for a first date!

Our similar reaction to the infamous campfire scene sealed the deal for Bill. He knew right then and there I was the one for him. It took me another week to realize I was smitten for life.

Unbeknownst to me, several weeks later, he drove the sixty miles to my father's home. After some awkward small talk and chit-chat, Bill mustered the courage and asked my dad, man to man, for my hand in marriage.

Somehow, my dad knew this big guy was the one for me, even though we had only known each other a short while. Dad was famous for looking, seeing, and *knowing* with his heart. He could determine a man's true character through the firmness of his handshake and if the man's eyes locked, straight on, eye-to-eye with his.

I think my dad had realized over the years, watching me grow and mature, I never fit the suburb mold, hard as I tried. Oh, sure, I could do it, but he knew deep within his heart, *my* deepest desire was to be a country girl.

I was a young woman who loved to wear overalls and hiking boots. I didn't have the desire for the frills of fashion or to mess with make-up. My dad knew I didn't mind getting my hands dirty. I loved chopping firewood and despised city traffic. I believe deep within my father's heart and soul, he *knew* I'd be in good hands—both God's and Bill's, *not* Allstate's™. ('Being in Good Hands' was a secret code between me and my dad—one of our heart-to-heart sayings we shared whenever times were tough.)

On a Sunday, two weeks after Bill talked with my father, at 4:15 pm, March 25, 1975, the larger-than-life, gorgeous wrestler gallantly knelt on bended knee in the bright-yellow kitchen where he had downed sodas and inhaled cookies prior to our study-date. He caught me off guard as he asked, "Will you marry me, to be my wife, the mother of my children, but most of all, my best friend, with God's help?" as he slipped a white sapphire ring on my left ring finger. It fit perfectly.

We waited two months to announce our engagement publicly, at his grandparents' 50th wedding anniversary party. It was a grand celebration, not to mention an honor Bill's Dutch grandfather and German grandmother highly regarded. I was welcomed with hugs and love all around.

We made a choice that day—no matter what we faced, or how hard times might get: NO wimping out!

With God's help, lots of laughter and with the tenets of Faith, Family, and *Fun*, we would hit life head on—together. No turning back.

4

LESSON OF THE RING

When Bill asked me to marry him, the engagement ring he slipped on my left ring finger was a family heirloom. It was a simple white sapphire with a gold band. Originally, it had been a gentleman's stick/lapel pin Bill's great-great grandfather wore. When his great-grandfather became engaged, his father passed the pin down to his son. The son had it made into an engagement ring for his future bride. A wonderful tradition began as it has continued to be passed down, generation to generation.

Sapphire is my birthstone which made the gift even more special.

It was a lovely show-piece, hard to miss as it glittered in dazzling sunlight and sparkled in natural indoor light. Here I was, a city-girl, engaged to a one-hundred-percent country boy. The ring was in stark contrast to me—a rather Plain Jane wall flower. Until this occasion, the scope of my jewelry was simple. I wore round, stud-type pierced earrings. No loops, no dangling-swirling objects hanging from my paternally inherited, elongated earlobes. Occasionally, I wore a basic silver necklace. There you have it. The un-voluminous extent of my accessorizing!

It was obvious people noticed the ring. Not only was it a lovely piece of jewelry… but *I* was wearing it!

Besides blushing a great deal when people commented, I had an additional conundrum. I was in the middle of my last semester of clinical fieldwork rotations as an occupational therapy student. My assignment was at a hospital. I was very much in the habit of *not* wearing a ring. Now I found myself regularly snagging my nylon stockings—a dress code requirement—on the beautiful ring which became an expensive problem to my meager college student's budget.

Another glitch I ran into was accidentally scratching a patient (or three) as I transferred them from their hospital bed to a wheelchair.

I became an expert at catching the ring on objects sticking out. It was accompanied by my equally clumsy technique of trying to extricate myself from whatever object I caught the ring on. It made for quite a spectacle. Sigh… what's a girl to do, but join the laughter at my expense.

The resolution to cause no further harm (to anyone—myself and stockings included) was to stop wearing the ring. It pained me immensely. Bill and I agreed the ring was only a symbol of our love, *not* the measure of our commitment to each other, or the measure of our love for each other. We *wanted* people to know we were engaged—that I was spoken for. To be honest, I *wanted* to show off the beautiful ring. But in reality, we didn't *need* the ring to announce our intentions, much less brag about it. So became the *Lesson of the Ring*: Is it a *need*…or a *want*?

We determined the best long-term solution to be had was to have matching wedding bands—*no* gems. We chose silver rings with a cross cut out of it. For us, it was a visual demonstration and reminder of our deep faith and our commitment to live in the grace of the One who had brought us together, 'til death do us part.

The sapphire ring forever symbolized a treasured life lesson. Early in our engagement, my first diagnosis of cancer was detected. I was just shy of being twenty-years-old. The reality of mounting medical bills, numerous time consuming appointments, and surgeries hadn't hit as yet. Yet over the years when reality *did* hit, we were prompted to revisit the *Lesson of the Ring* many times in our marriage.

One might think the moral of said lesson of the ring was to do no harm. Au contraire!

The impact and magnitude of The *Lesson of the Ring* brought a question into our lives and marriage that continues to be one of our major life compasses:

"*Is it a True Need or Want?*"

The significant lesson brought us to our knees on more than one occasion.

The question has held through wearing—or not *wearing*—a ring. It held us steady during lean days of financial challenges and medical mazes, or as we wandered tantalizing grocery aisles. When we were still newlyweds, temptations often struck hard.

Our chosen professions did not pay as well as the professions our siblings chose. It stung when they could jet off for tropical vacations, or live in homes we could only dream about. We felt the societal pressure to keep up with our friends who were upgrading their vehicles to the newest model. We knew the tactics of the enemy could be subtle. So, when the taunts plagued us, we were ready to hear God gently remind us to hold each other accountable, and asking each other, is this a *true need* or a *want*?

Our choice? We chose to live in DIY fixer-uppers and to stick with our blue, 1968, sixteen passenger van. People knew we were coming as eight-track cassettes blared away as we be-bopped up and down the local streets or flying on the freeway!

To this day, particularly when I go on girl's day out or on an irresistible shopping trip, I still find myself asking, "Is this adorable outfit a *true need* or is it a *want*?"

More times than not, it is a "*want*."

Because of this phrase—this lesson—we have been able to give and share with others in *true* need. We have been able to help friends through tragedies, illnesses, unexpected or unbudgeted catastrophes, and/or finding themselves over their heads in debt. Yes, we've even helped others work on a financial plan when they foolishly made the choice for *want* over *need*. We've shown other couples how to establish The *Lesson of the Ring* in their relationship. We challenge them not to wimp out—to hold each other accountable, to love each other enough to ask each other, "Is this a *true need* or *want*?"

My heart is full, thinking of what this lesson has taught us. The benefits reaped have been countless. I smile, knowing the sapphire-heirloom-ring will be passed down through yet another generation.

5

PROMISES KEPT

Most of us are familiar with traditional wedding vows saying something like, *I (name), take thee (name), to be my wedded husband/wife.*

The next line usually goes, *To have and to hold, from this day forward, for better or worse, for richer or poorer, in sickness and in health, to love and to cherish, until death do us part, according to God's Word, I promise.*

March 27, 1976, was a blissful day. Bill and I were so excited to celebrate our wedding. At last! We were able to say our vows in the church we attended during our college days. It was a historic, 1890-era church, complete with a steeple and bell tower. The bell tolled daily at noon, each Sunday morning as services began, and on special occasions such as a wedding. The interior was adorned with stunning stained-glass windows and hand-carved, high-backed, late 1800's-era pews with embroidered kneelers at the altar.

The acoustics in the century old church were amazing—especially when music from the enormous pipe organ filled the air with hymns and music of Bach or Beethoven. I especially loved it when Bill let *his* voluminous multi-range "pipes" fill the church as he sang during the hymns of worship. It was a perfect setting to start our happily-ever-after marriage.

This church was special as this was where Bill and I began our personal relationship and journey with God together. We both wanted God to be first in our life *and* marriage. We desired a *personal* relationship with God. Not just a Sunday-morning-go-to-church relationship. We were blessed to have married couples in the church who mentored us, friends in *Young Life*, and campus activities helping us understand what it meant to have God first in your life—your best friend, your heart being His home.

In mere moments Bill and I joined many couples before us and repeat the familiar wedding vows. Never mind our best man dropped his powder blue tux in the mud.

No bother one of the bridesmaids forgot her dress—an hour away from the church. She arrived back to the church with milli-seconds to spare before she was to walk down the aisle.

And where was the organist? The prelude was scheduled to begin at 6:45 p.m. as guests arrived. With a quick phone call, we quickly discovered she thought the wedding started at 8:00 p.m. rather than 7:30 p.m.

"Okay, Care," I told myself, *"Take a breath. No more tears. So what if a few things have gone wrong?"*

I sighed. *"Today of all days, I wish Mom was here."*

My next thought was a reprimand. *"Care: Mom is here! She just has the best seat of all. In Heaven! And above all, remember God has chosen Bill—just for you!"*

As if on cue, a dozen red roses arrived in the bride's dressing room. The card simply said: "Lady, I'm yours forever – Ummers: +++" (Ummers was our code word for a kiss and +++ meant I'll love you forever and more.)

I melted into a puddle of tears. Again.

As I did my best to regain composure, I took in a deep breath, filling my lungs with the fragrance of the roses. Bill had never sent me flowers before. We had diligently stuck to our *need* vs. *want* motto. But Bill knew, right then, it was not only a *need* (for me) but a *want*, for him. Joy replaced the tears, filling my heart. Bill. I was going to be his.

In a matter of moments, it was time to walk down the aisle. My dad patted my hand and gave me his signature grin. A peace settled over me. I knew God was in control. I was in Good Hands.

Rushed footsteps sounded to my right. The wedding coordinator whispered something in my ear. *What?*! Bill's four-year-old nephew got his head stuck in the railing slats on the stairs leading to the altar?

"*Take another deep breath Care, don't panic. Someone else will take care of him,*" I told myself.

Dad held my hand and squeezed it tight as we walked down the aisle. As he transferred my hand from his to Bill's, he firmly clasped his hands over ours. He gave Bill a sparkling, blue-eyed wink. The wink was an assurance Dad knew Bill's love for me was a forever and always kind of love, protecting and cherishing me.

The priest asked us to repeat those time-treasured vows after him.

Bill began. He forgot the words "in sickness and in health."

The priest whispered, "Just keep going, Bill. Don't worry about it."

Then it was my turn. I repeated my vows—with *all* the words—and soon we were blissfully waltzing down the aisle of the historic, stained-glassed church as Mr. and Mrs.

Needless to say, over the years, we have wondered more than a time or ten, what might have happened if Bill had remembered to add the "*in sickness and in health*" phrase in his vows. Only God knew.

With my fourteen battles with cancer, being hit by a drunk driver, experiencing a brain bleed leaving me learning to walk, talk, and do daily activities all over, plus becoming bionic with my arms, legs, back, and head screwed, bolted, and glued together, and now a brain tumor, it is a miracle our marriage has survived.

Bill has always had me and *held* me, for over four decades now. We definitely have the "*for richer and poorer*" part down with all the medical bills. We have lived the "*for better or worse*" part with the medical challenges and adversity, plus opportunities and adventures we've encountered. *Loving* and *cherishing* each other as best friends have been the foundation of our daily lives, all with God's help.

When I tease him for leaving out those crucial words, he reminds me while I have accomplished a great deal over the years—from being an occupational therapist, getting my Master's degree in Education in 1997, helping develop *Wheels For The World™* for *Joni and Friends™*, being named one of the "Top 5 Business Woman in America" in 2000 by Wyndham Resorts, American Airlines and Liz Claiborne, and becoming the first Alaskan to be named *Hero of Hope* for the American Cancer Society™ (2013), I have *not* done very well at the *dying* portion of the "*until death do us part*." Even after 120+ surgeries and injuries! (Being given CPR and revived twice doesn't count, he says.)

We *did* promise to stay together. No regrets.

Many people question Bill why he didn't walk away years ago. After all, many marriages when faced with chronic illnesses, financial challenges, debt, death, and more, end up in divorce.

Bill's reply is always the same. "I love her – she's my best friend besides my wife. And when I make a promise, I don't break it. *Especially* to God! End of story.

Bill's reply is one more example of how to handle life's daily challenges and battles—no matter what. With courage we can face life head on, walking with God and each other. When we live our life in faith, with hope and much love, there *are* no regrets.

6

NO ONE TOLD US ABOUT *THIS* PART

After our honeymoon, Bill and I realized our lives were in store for some major adjustments for both of us.

To start with, I had to complete my senior year in Occupational Therapy, including two off-campus fieldwork internships. My psychiatric/mental health field-work experience allowed me to stay in the region with only a forty-five-minute commute from home. My second internship posed a different situation. Before we had uttered our wedding vows, I had been chosen as one of only a handful of recent O.T. graduates from across the country to do physical disability/rehabilitation field work at the prestigious Mayo Clinic, in Rochester, Minnesota.

After much talk and prayer, we *knew* I couldn't turn down the Mayo Clinic opportunity. But it also wasn't practical for both of us to move from the Pacific Northwest to Minnesota for only six months. *Someone* had to work to pay the bills. Internships and fieldwork experiences rarely gave stipends, much less travel expenses, room or board.

So off I went, all by my lonesome. The months dragged on for what seemed like an eternity. To this day, it is the longest we've ever been apart in our forty-plus years together. But the experiences, the networking, the life-long friendships made, plus the lessons of long-distance love were far from wasted.

On the first day of the field work internship, the supervisor of the Rehab Unit held an orientation meeting with the new thera-pists. He spent the morning meeting outlining expectations, the daily schedule, and routines. At the conclusion of the meeting was a reminder of the recently revised number of hours and scheduled dates required to complete the internship.

Revised as in—the day before. I was heartbroken.

You see, the internship started September 1st and was to con-tinue for four months. December 31st was the scheduled end date. No exceptions were allowed.

I realized it meant not being home for our first Christmas together as husband and wife.

The thought was devastating.

I brought my conundrum to my no-nonsense supervisor. He once again reiterated and made it *exceptionally* clear: there would be *no* exceptions to the revised schedule.

I did the only thing I knew to do… I prayed. (Besides crying myself to sleep many nights.)

To make a little extra money, I offered my time as a babysitter to the staff. Since Bill and I were so far apart, I was available nights and weekends. Imagine my total shock when my no-non-sense supervisor asked if I could watch his kids on several occa-sions. They were great kids! We had fun playing board games, making holiday themed cookies, and watching movies together. We even hatched a plan to surprise their mother on her birthday by *totally* cleaning the house, bathrooms and all, *and* made her a birthday cake—frosted and decorated as only a five-year-old and seven-year-old can.

One day, about half-way through my field work internship, my supervisor sternly called me into his office.

Shaking in my boots and my knees knocking, I wondered what I might have done wrong. I tapped on his office door.

He signaled me to come in.

As I walked into his office, he asked me to close the door behind me.

My thoughts swirled in my head. *"Boy, I must have really messed up!"*

He caught me off guard when he began speaking in an unfamiliar, softened tone of voice. Modestly, he shared his gratitude to me for my willingness to babysit his children. He shared how impressed he and his wife were in the many thoughtful and fun ways I interacted with his children.

"Someday, you will make a great mother."

His words of praise really touched my heart.

"I am willing to make my first ever exception to my no-nonsense rules. But you will have to be willing to work extra hours in the evenings and/or weekends on the Rehabilitation Unit to build up the required number of hours to successfully complete and pass the physical disabilities/surgical internship."

I'm sure my jaw must have dropped.

"If you agree, I am willing to let you leave at noon on December 24th. With a little luck and no flight delays, you can make it home in time for your first Christmas with your husband."

I was in shock. Words failed me when I needed them most. Finally, I found my voice. "Yes! Yes! I'd be *more* than willing to accept the offer!" A grin the size of Alaska must have broken out on my face.

"Well, then… it's settled. Now wipe the silly grin off your face and get back to work," his stern no-nonsense tone of voice returning.

Talk about God being in the details and answering the cries of my heart! I could hear Jesus' words and my dad's voice both uttering a phrase used many times in my growing up years. *"O, ye of little faith."*

Leave it to Old Man Winter to try and stop my reunion with

Bill from becoming a reality. Long holiday lines at the airport—coupled with snow related weather delays, re-routes and cancelled flights—greeted me at the Minneapolis-St. Paul airport. I had no other choice but to wait. I joined the others and entered the long line at the gate attendant's desk. I set my backpack and one carry-on piece of luggage down, draped my down parka over them, and plopped on top of the pile.

I was exhausted and longing to be with Bill. Disappointment filled my thoughts. The delays were out of my control and in God's hands.

My flight home ended up being delayed *four* times.

I so wanted to spend our first Christmas as husband and wife together.

I tried hard to keep a positive attitude and not wimp out. But it was not easy.

At long last, several hours later, my flight number was called to start boarding. I found my assigned seat and settled in, but I still couldn't bring myself to think there was *any* way I could be home by Christmas morning. My problem was I was *thinking…* not *believing*.

Christmas miracles *do* occur, and not only in sappy holiday movies.

With the two-hour time difference, I arrived at my airport destination gate at 11:58 p.m. Just in time for our first Christmas as a married couple.

"*O ye of little faith…*" Jesus' words once more echoed in my heart as I leapt into my husband's out-stretched arms.

Imagine my surprise when a copy of the front page of the Christmas-morning edition of the *Minneapolis Star* newspaper arrived in our mailbox several days later, from friends in Minnesota. There, smack dab on the front page, was a quarter-page photo of *me*! All of my weariness, disappointment, and loneliness were captured in the photo. My fist rested under my chin as I sat on my backpack in the long line.

The caption read: "*Coming, Going, and Waiting.*" It was an article about the lengthy holiday lines, weather and flight delays at the Minneapolis-St. Paul airport.

Apparently, as I was sitting and waiting at my departure gate at the airport, I had been totally oblivious to the *click-click-click* sound of a news reporter's camera. My eyes were downcast. I was brooding and longing to be in Bill's arms. I had become more than weary, worn, and disappointed. Faith was far from being my first 'go-to'… but thankfully, it *was* God's.

I never set out to be on a front page photo of Minneapolis' largest newspaper. I simply wanted to get home for Christmas.

Once again God's will and God's way prevailed. He's all about the details and timing.

7

I DIDN'T KNOW CASTRATING A BULL WAS IN THE "I DO"

Growing up in the suburbs, I was raised with the philosophy: cleanliness is next to Godliness. May I just say? That hardly describes life on a farm. Soon after my Occupational Therapy internships were completed and my National Certification Board tests were taken—and passed—my husband and I settled into renting a small apartment in the town where he grew up. It was a cozy 700 square-foot apartment, located in the front inside corner of a 2000 square-foot, metal-sided, combination apartment-garage-horse stall-barn with five fenced acres for cows or horses. The long driveway from our new abode was directly across from the farm where Bill spent his growing up years from the time he was four until just before his senior year in high school. Hmm… do I detect a *God*incidence?!

After Bill's folks sold their farm and moved into town in 1972, Bill's mother and her best friend and former next-farm-over neighbor, continued their weekly Sunday morning coffee klatch. Mom arrived at the farm promptly at 9 a.m. They consumed copious cups of coffee as they updated each other on the latest comings and goings around the area.

The weekly ritual was still going strong when we moved into our apartment and mini-farm in 1977. Since we now lived only a short distance away from the farm, I was occasionally invited to join them. Oy vey! Consequently, I learned *nothing* Bill and I did was sacred. These two farmer's wives kept tabs on *everyone*! We could barely sneeze without hearing about it!

Mom heard about our new washer and dryer being delivered before it ever arrived down our driveway. Not even my dad's stories about his work at the regional telephone company about transitioning from party lines to private lines—and how everyone knew everyone else's business—could prepare me for situations like this. It became obvious the days of party-line phone gossip were just too hard for these delightful, farmers' wives to give up!

There were other differences between city life and small-town life I was not prepared for. Before getting married, my daily chores revolved around commuting in rush hour traffic to and from work in Seattle, meals out with friends, and strolls through a Farmers Market during my summer work lunch hour. Now, my daily chores included activities far beyond my knowledge base.

Keeping up a mini-farm included feeding chickens, collecting their daily fresh-laid eggs, cleaning the chicken coop, tending a garden, and raising an intimidating and quite belligerent thirty-five pound Tom turkey plus three turkey hens. I even learned how—and helped—to butcher chickens and turkeys for future holiday meals or to have on hand in the freezer. Oh! I almost forgot to mention making sure the cattle water tank was full.

This became my new normal. I stayed in shape not by going to the gym, but by learning how to drive and operate farm equipment, bucking and lifting bales of hay onto a trailer, then throwing and stacking those bales in the hay-barn. Lots of animals needed the hay—especially the beef cows we were raising.

One of the bull calves we fondly named George. Bill showed me how to rubber-band castrate the bulls when they were small. I was tentative and a bit more than squeamish about helping. I learned this was standard practice, not to mention one of the easiest and least painful methods of castrating a young bull calf, especially if they were being raised for future meals. I did my best to not pass out, if only by sheer will. I can't say the same about the tears trickling down my face when George bellowed and bawled out a loud, mournful cry as the band was snapped in place.

I enjoyed bottle feeding George and chasing him when he was small. Bill warned me not to get too attached to him, reminding me the day was not far off when George became a part of our Sunday dinners.

All too soon, the day came to butcher George. Our local butcher arrived with his truck, hoist, and needed tools. He looked down at George and said to Bill, "You *did* know he still has one testicle, don't you?"

Bill nodded as he told the butcher, "Yeah, I didn't get the band tight enough. We fondly gave him the nickname "One Nut.""

We gave the go ahead to butcher him anyway.

But the butcher gave us another option. "You know, if you finish castrating him and let him go another month, the meat will be tenderer. What do you say? It's what I'd do if it were me."

Bill weighed the options and went with the butcher's suggestion.

"Guess I'll see you next month then," he said. He put away his tools and waved goodbye as he drove off.

Rubber-band castration was reserved for young bull calves. Since George was long past that stage, a surgical procedure needed to be performed. To save ourselves a hefty veterinarian bill, we used the opportunity to invite local high school agriculture students to get some hands on, experiential learning.

When the day to finish castrating George arrived, I mustered as much courage as a city girl had. The Ag students and their teacher gathered out at the hay barn as Bill brought George in. Before beginning, the Ag teacher assured his students (and me!)

this was an easy-peasy fifteen-minute procedure. The only pain George might feel was the pinprick of a local anesthetic numbing shot.

Once the shot was out of the way, Bill lifted and held George's tail up, while two of the students firmly held his head. The Ag teacher then demonstrated how a surgical castration on a bull was performed.

One might think, after working on both animal and human cadavers in OT school, watching a surgical procedure was sure to be no problem. But, as the procedure started, I first turned ghostly white, followed by a garish green color. Or so I'm told. To make matters worse, the Ag teacher called over to me, "Hey Care, come here! Hold out your hands for a minute—I need your help!"

Holding my hands out as requested, I suddenly heard a *plop*! I felt the weight of something I didn't want to acknowledge.

The testicle had been dropped into my hands as the teacher continued, "And don't you *dare* drop it, that's my dinner. I *love* Rocky Mountain Oysters!"

As sure as the day is long, I was the expense of many jokes.

I never imagined castrating a bull came with the simple "I do" of our wedding vows. Come to think of it…there have been many facets of married life not detailed in our wedding vows. But that's the beauty of marriage.

Though I still have some of my city-girl traits, Bill dubbed me a full-fledged "country girl" that day, earning my title after helping with George. Through the years I have come to appreciate my husband's full-farm-boy, country insights. He sees beyond *what is*, to *what he can make of it*, to *what will be*. The ability to see beyond the surface has been a recurring blessing I know I can rely on every single day.

Bill may not always see the road ahead, but he has always been aware of when it's been time to move forward. He knows the value of living one day at a time. Bill is a firm believer and shares his personal view that: "People who live for tomorrow die wishing. People who live for yesterday die discouraged. But people who live for today have no regrets, for they are living in the very moment." Bill's intentional willingness to listen when God speaks to him, has never led him, or us, astray.

Not long after George's castration and the butchering the Thanksgiving turkeys, our lease on the mini-farm was up,

It was time to move forward – to a neighboring small town. We were elated when we found an old farm house to rent on one acre – and included a small, detached barn.

What's even more amazing, the house we'd be renting was next door to Bill's cousin. This cousin was one of the talented and gifted people who mentored Bill in the carpentry trade.

8

GATHERING WISDOM

Growing up in the late 1950's to the early 1970's, Bill and I lived under our parents' roofs. Rules were meant to be followed, and respect was an unspoken given.

You *knew* if you used a four-letter-word (a swear word) or other unacceptable speech, you were sure to get your mouth cleansed by one of your parents with a toothbrush and a bar of soap. It was a society-approved form of punishment of the day. If not adhered to, the duly doled out consequence was performed. While it failed physical harm, save the obnoxious—and quite possibly intended—lingering after-taste, the lesson was learned!

High expectations created an environment to allow us to rise to the occasion. Our parents were helping us to develop values serving us well in the future. Their hope for us was to learn there were *always* consequences for choices made—good or bad. Bill and I have done our best to impart these lessons and more, to our kids and others entrusted to us.

First and foremost was the importance of faith in God, and the gifts and passions He has bestowed on each of us—as individuals and as newly-weds. The lessons were especially helpful as we ventured into our married life and beyond. We learned lessons of respect, honesty and integrity. We learned about the importance of your word, meaningful two-way verbal communication, and hard work.

I continued to follow my chosen profession of occupational therapy. At first, Bill combined his perfected hands-on abilities acquired from growing up on a farm and picking up local jobs. He could usually find work driving trucks, manning heavy equipment, applying mechanical and electrical expertise, and basic carpentry and fix-it skills. He put other skills to use he had acquired from majoring in education in college.

Many of Bill's jobs were seasonal, which occasionally left our budget in limbo. When push eventually came to shove financially, he realized he needed guaranteed full-time work to support what we hoped someday soon, led to a growing family.

Bill made the decision to commit and focus on the carpentry trade. As with most careers, he started as low man on the totem-pole. Carpentry soon became not just a full-time, year round job but a true passion. He discovered his gift of common-sense ways and problem-solving are not so common. He found the hard work and chores from his days on the farm had honed his skills and abilities, and crossed over into carpentry. His years of participating in competitive sports and coaching found their place in carpentry as well. There were rules and regulations galore needing to abide by.

Bill *loved* carpentry and the sweat and labor around it. It was fun to him. The more creative he could be the better. Over the years he built custom homes, worked on union commercial jobs, fast-food restaurants, waste water treatment facilities, home remodels, and "can-you-figure-this-problem-out?" jobs. As the farm slogan goes, "he was in hog heaven!"

As our newlywed finances leveled out, we began to seriously talk about adding to our family. While yes, getting pregnant was on our minds and in our hearts, until it happened, we promised each other not to worry. We continued our young married life on our mini-farm and working jobs we were both passionate about.

We were active in our local church and led the youth group. In our spare time, we enjoyed weekend camping and hiking trips, sprinkled in with weekly get-togethers with friends.

Weeks turned into months. The months turned into over a year. Why wasn't I pregnant yet? While we trusted God and knew His timing to be perfect, we couldn't help but be impatient at times. We so badly wanted children.

One morning in 1978, I felt a wave of nausea come over me. It didn't feel like the flu, but I couldn't pinpoint where it was coming from. Could it be? Was *this* what morning-sickness felt like? For three mornings in a row, the waves of nausea hit. It was hard not to get overly excited about the possibility of being pregnant. Over the counter pregnancy test kits were not on the market yet, so if you thought you might be pregnant, you had to get a blood test for confirmation. For us, doctor visits cost money not in our monthly budget, unless absolutely necessary.

On the fourth day, my belly fully flip-flopped. I couldn't put it off any longer. It was time to go get the test. While I was waiting for the results to see if I was pregnant, my mind went wild with anticipation. A radiology technician entered the room and told me the doctor ordered an ultrasound, and I was instructed to come with her. Ultrasound complete, I returned to the patient room for more waiting. When the nurse finally came in, I jumped to my feet and excitedly asked, "Well, am I?"

Before she could answer, our family physician walked into the room.

Uh-oh… I wasn't expecting to see *him*, my thoughts went all over the place, my heart beating a bit faster.

Doc Z—as he was fondly known—was a big, kind, burly, teddy-bear type of man. The kind you see in old Western movies playing the role of country doctor. He told me to sit back down. In his country-doctor style, he clasped my hands in one of his. With his other hand he patted my knee and said, "I'm so sorry. I know you and Bill were hoping you are pregnant… as were we."

Sorry… for what? We had *plenty* of days ahead of us to have kids if this turned out to be some sort of flu bug and not the first trimester of being pregnant.

He went on. "I want you to go over to the hospital, right away. I am admitting you for observation for at least the next twenty-four hours. No, you are not pregnant. And, you don't have the flu, either. I'm afraid this is more serious. Because of your exposure to the drug DES, there is a strong possibility you have something very wrong with your left ovary. I want to run more tests and watch you. I'm so sorry." He asked if he could pray with me before I left for the hospital.

My mouth went dry. I couldn't speak. I wanted Bill to be there with me, instead of his mother who was in the outer waiting room. I nodded yes. He began to pray. In his prayer, he asked for a covering of comfort and peace for Bill and me. He pleaded for wisdom, skill and discernment for all involved with my care. He closed the prayer uttering a thanksgiving in advance. He didn't just *talk*, Doc Z *walked his talk*.

Finding my voice I looked up at the doctor, "Thank you for your words of wisdom and for praying with me."

Weak-kneed, I slowly stood up. Tendrils of icy fear began to creep into the crevasses and depths of my heart and soul as I walked out to the waiting room. I knew we were headed into uncharted territory and the *only* way we'd make it through was to surround ourselves with the ones who loved us deeply—the ones who carried the torches of wisdom, discernment, experience and faith.

And most importantly, cling to God.

9

DOUBT

As I made my way to the waiting room, I signaled Bill's mom, pointing to the outside door leading to her car. I didn't speak a word. Hot, stinging tears streamed down my face. Once outside, in between sobs, I choked out what the doctor had said.

"Oh, sweetie," Bill's mom said in her loving way.

I was so relieved she didn't say anything more. No "I'm sorry" or "It will all work out." I honestly believe she didn't know *what* to say. I knew she could see the disappointment on my face. I couldn't hide my fear as my trembling hands twisted and turned a damp tissue around my little finger. We drove the five blocks to the community hospital in silence.

Once settled in a hospital room, Bill's mother told me she'd get in touch with Bill, even if it meant going to his job site. We didn't have cell phones back then.

Bill rushed to the hospital as soon as he got the news. He was a grimy, dirty mess. So concerned about me, he hadn't taken time to wash his carpentry calloused hands. He awkwardly attempted to make small talk as he paced around the room.

I knew his distain of hospitals. He was of the opinion you don't go to the hospital unless you are in dire straits or close to death. His discomfort and pacing for hours started to get to me. I suggested he go home and I promised to call him if I needed anything. He could stop by on his way to work the next day. A visible look of relief came over his face.

"Are you sure?" he asked.

"There's nothing *you* can do right now, so go get some supper, take a shower, and get a good night's sleep. I'm in good hands, with people you have grown up with as nurses, technicians, and the doctors. Now go!"

He leaned over and kissed me, then prayed with me and kissed me again, leaving a small sawdust souvenir on the crisp white hospital bed sheets. "Ummers, Lady," he said as he walked out the door.

The hours after Bill left were filled with blood tests, x-rays, exams, and the usual busy routine of a hospital. As my pain increased, so did the administration of pain medication, causing me to doze off and on.

Somewhere around 10:00 p.m., buzzers from the machines I was hooked up to went crazy. A flurry of nurses streamed into my room. One of them barked, "Call the doctor—*stat!*"

As minutes ticked by, I started to become unresponsive, slipping in and out of consciousness. Doc Z was summoned to my bedside to assess the situation. He motioned the head nurse to follow him to the nurse's station.

"Call Bill and tell him to get here *right away*. I think we are losing her. I don't know where the bleeding is coming from. But *don't* tell Bill *anything*. Just get him here – *NOW!*"

We lived about fifteen miles from the hospital. Bill made it to the hospital in ten minutes. You do the math as to how fast he was driving—and add the fact he had to get dressed first, since he had just gone to bed!

The doctor met Bill as he flew in the front doors of the hospital. Doc Z explained the full situation, as they knew it at the moment. He also told Bill he didn't want *me* to know I was hemorrhaging. The team didn't know where it was coming from. I needed emergency exploratory surgery. But before they could do surgery, he needed Bill to drive to the blood bank, forty-five miles away, and pick up several pints of blood. The personnel at the blood bank were expecting him. The doctor told Bill to take a friend to be with him "just in case."

Time seemed to drag by for me as my pain increased. Before long, two nurses came in to prepare me for surgery. I was in so much pain; I didn't even ask what the surgery was for.

As I was being wheeled down the corridor, the late-night drop-of-a-pin quiet was abruptly shattered. Two solidly built men came sauntering down the hospital hall, two bags of blood in their hands, belting out a loud, boisterous song in their tenor and bass voices. Their uncharacteristic, jovial demeanor, under the circumstances, bounced off the hospital corridor walls.

"Oh, Lord, please tell me that's not Bill and Leroy." I mused before I totally blacked out from the powerful medication given to me.

Later, Bill sheepishly asked me to forgive his and Leroy's loud behavior. It was hard not to chuckle as I forgave him. After all, I had been under the influence when they serenaded the hospital staff and other patients. I'm sure what I heard was probably very different!

Once in surgery, the team found where the bleeding was coming from. Unfortunately, my left ovary literally exploded as they removed it. The three surgeons were able to see a major genetic deformation in the right ovary as well. Then, to make things even more interesting, the surgeons discovered I had two *full* uteruses, plus the start of a third uterus—a common side effect of the DES drug; all were part of a rare form of cancer. Since the surgery was an emergency and I had lost a fair amount of blood, they decided to wait and see how I recovered before addressing the other anomalies they had discovered.

I asked the surgical team, "Will we still be able to have kids?" One surgeon said *no*, one surgeon said *yes*, and the third surgeon in on the emergency procedure said *maybe*. The latter said, "After healing a few weeks, you can get back to trying—we just don't know for sure if your body will support a pregnancy."

Only God knew the answer…and only time will tell.

10

FROM DREAMS AND DREAD
TO DISMAY AND DELIGHT

Following the third surgeon's encouraging advice, we *did* try to get pregnant over the next year. During long drives or late hour pillow talks we also began to talk Plan B options if we *couldn't* get pregnant. We agreed it might be best to at least start researching adoption.

There were so many options to consider, so many things to think and pray about. Did we want a newborn? Did we want to go through an agency? Did we want an open adoption? Did we want a boy or a girl? What about twins? What about adopting a child from another country or a child with a disability? A friend asked us if we considered being foster parents.

Four more months passed. We still weren't pregnant. So, we finally decided to start the process of applying for the adoption of a newborn. We filled out mounds and mountains of paperwork from numerous private and state agencies. Some of the applications were so specific—to the point of intrusive—it seemed like they wanted to know how many times we sneezed backward in the second grade!

One question in particular tickled our funny bone was, "When the two of you disagree and/or have an argument, how do you settle it?" The question threw us for a loop. In all honesty, we didn't ever really argue. We might loudly *explain* why one or the other of us might be right, but we truly didn't argue! How *do* we answer the question, we wondered?

"I've got it!" Bill said. "Let's pick a pretend argument and see if we can actually argue - maybe then we'll know how to answer!"

We tried our best, but every time we tried we ended up in hysterics. We told the agencies the truth: when we disagree, we make the time-out hand signal and stop—right where we are. We sit down, verbally agreeing to disagree. We honestly listened to each other's side, and then we joined hands and prayed, asking God for wisdom and direction and forgiving each other. After ending the prayer, we would engage in a big long embrace, kiss and make up. When we followed our own rule, making up was *not* hard to do.

Over time, application after application came back denied. One agency would say we didn't have enough income. Another would reject our style of argument resolution. Several agencies thought we were too young or we hadn't been married long enough. The most ludicrous rejection—in our opinion—was the one stating it would be improper for Bill to be the stay-at-home-parent. At the time, I was able to make a higher salary than Bill at the time. *Men* in the 1970's weren't deemed worthy or capable enough to be the stay-at-home-parent.

The shifting sands of time. Forty years later, news reports lament that there are not enough men involved in child-care or kid's lives.

"Pish-tush," I used a phrase my mother used when she was disgruntled, not agreeing with an action or outcome of a situation.

One night after we read another rejection letter, we joined hands to pray. We told God if He wants us to adopt or have a child in our life, He would have to make it happen. We don't have the financial means to pay for a private adoption (a private agency adoption cost quoted to us was $40,000 for a newborn at the time.) We keep getting rejection letters from social service agencies, even though we have impeccable records and references. We don't know what else to do –except to say it's all Yours, God."

Bill and I have shared many times we think the prayer and conversation we had with God that night was exactly what He was waiting for. He was waiting for us to come to the end of ourselves so He could move in ways only He can.

Unexpectedly, about two weeks later we got a telephone call from a physician at our medical clinic. He asked us if we were still considering adoption. We said we were ready to adopt, but we had hit dead ends with all the applications. He told us there *might* be a possible private, person-to-person, anonymous adoption coming up through the local hospital. He inquired if we were interested?

"Were we interested? Of course, we are interested!" I exclaimed.

He said he'd tell the hospital administrators in charge of our decision to move forward. The doctor told me hospital officials will be in contact with us in four to five months, as the projected birth time got closer. After hanging up the phone we couldn't contain our joy. We jumped up and down, shouting, "*Thank you, Lord!*" until our voices were hoarse.

The hard part was we were not to tell anyone... *anyone.*

The months seemed like an eternity. Then one evening, we got the call.

"Get ready! It looks like the adoption is a go! You have three weeks to get ready before the baby is due!" The doctor on the other end of the telephone said.

The next three weeks were a whirlwind. We were both still working, so our evenings were filled with fixing up a nursery, buying *cloth* diapers (no disposable diapers back then!) and other baby items. We counted down the days. The phone rang. It was the doctor. I was trying to contain my excitement.

"Care?" he started. "Umm... I'm so sorry to have to tell you, but the birth mother decided to keep the baby."

Silence.

I didn't know what to say.

"Well, Doc, we *knew* this could be a possibility," I choked out, trying to hide my dismay.

I felt sucker-punched. Didn't this woman know the pain she was inflicting? Didn't she know our dream was now turned to a disappointing nightmare because of her decision?

"Care, don't give up," the doctor encouraged me. "We still *might* have another baby available in a few weeks. Don't get your hopes up, but if it works out, you will not be able to be at the hospital (it was where I also worked as an OT) as soon as the mother goes into labor. It's to protect everyone, for confidentiality and liability reasons."

I let out a long breath.

"Can you and Bill stay ready, stay strong, and hang in there?"

I assured the doctor we could hang in there, even though at the moment we were sorely disheartened.

The doctor related he couldn't give me any more details, as much as he wanted to, but this was the first *totally* anonymous newborn adoption through the hospital in twelve years. Every action, every conversation had to be done legally and by the book. Even the staff could not know whose baby it was (the mother was to be given a pseudo-name) or who the adoptive parents were to be. Once delivered, the infant was to be wrapped in the *opposite* color of baby bunting to further conceal any facts from being leaked.

We agreed to all the terms, including the same financial agreement as the first offer of adoption that fell through—namely, we were responsible for paying the mother's pre-natal care as well as hospital and legal fees. While those fees were *far* less than going through an agency—private or public—it meant setting up a monthly payment plan.

Two weeks later, in the middle of the night, the phone rang. Bill leapt out of bed. He ran to the kitchen where the land-line telephone hung on the wall. He answered.

I heard him say, "Yep… yep. I got it. Thanks. Good Night."

He hung the phone up and crawled back into bed, pulling the covers up over himself.

"Who were you talking to?" I groggily asked.

"It was the Doc…we have a ba…" he stopped mid-sentence.

Bill *shot* out of bed and started shouting, "I'm a *dad!*"

He continued: "We have a baby girl! We have a baby girl!"

His words finally sank in and my heart felt like it was bursting through my chest as Bill drew me into his bear-hug embrace.

The legality of anonymity of the birth-mother had been kept. Staying within the legal boundaries, after three, *long*, agonizing days, we got to hold our little bundle in our arms and the hospital staff could know who the adoptive parents were. When we held our daughter for the first time, the staff of the hospital surrounded us. Word had spread like wildfire. Imagine our surprise when balloons, a cake, and gifts rolled up on a hospital cart.

After multiple photos were taken, best wishes and parental advice given, the enormity of the situation started to feel a bit overwhelming. The doctor recognized the overcome, almost dazed look on Bill's and my faces and told us, "Get out of here, you three! You can open the gifts when you get home. Take your little miracle angel home!"

We didn't need to be told twice. Home we went. We were complete. We had a baby girl. Life was good.

Thirty years passed before we heard many of the specifics behind the adoption. Only God could orchestrate and execute the infinite details and elements. We had been oblivious to how many people in the community were involved to make the adoption possible. One more affirmation God's timing is perfect. He has a plan and a purpose for our lives, and sometimes He waits for us to come to the end of ourselves so His plan for us can come to fruition. He had known this little one before she was ever in her mother's womb. He counted the very number of hairs on her head. He numbered her days, and trusted us to raise her to know Him, and she did.

When our little bundle was only three months old, I quickly recognized what the nauseous, belly flip-flop symptoms meant. Right away, I called the medical clinic. They put me on hold. The next voice I heard was Doc Z's. His voice boomed over the telephone line: "Get to the Emergency Room, *now!*"

Luckily, Bill was home—not only to drive me, but to make arrangements for someone to watch our infant daughter.

I was right. Within thirty minutes of arriving at the hospital, I was being wheeled into emergency surgery. My right ovary was beginning to rupture. My nemesis of DES related cancer returned. This time the verdict was final. I had to have a hysterectomy.

Being able to conceive on our own was never to be. Knowing the experience of being pregnant even with all its nuances was not to be. The Dutch birth blood-line of the family name had come to an end. While I knew I wasn't a failure to Bill, or to his family, it still hurt. I was disappointed and discouraged. Yet at the same time, I was so very grateful for the birth mother of our now three-month-old, for our families, for the physicians and nurses, our community, and most importantly to God, for lovingly showing us, once again, He is in *all* the details, and His timing is perfect.

Through the heartache of infertility and the possibility of adoption, we learned what it meant to come to the end of ourselves and to trust God. Even when we experienced dismay and the effects the drug DES had on my body, we *knew* God was with us.

God promises He will be with you, as well, through the tough and disappointing times. Just remember: when you come to the end of yourself (like us!) it often makes the hurt go away a bit faster.

11

DELINQUENTS

The national economic downfall of the late 1970's and early 1980's eventually caught up to us, when our wee one was only six-months-old. Carpentry was in a slump. We held out for as long as we could. But when the cold, hard facts of not being able to pay our monthly bills on two part-time incomes became a reality, it forced us to take one of our first leaps of faith as a married couple. Holding our parents' core values and high expectation lessons close to our heart, we moved away from all things familiar to us.

We left mini-farming and living close to family and friends. My heart-strings tugged as I left my first professional job as an occupational therapist at the hospital and school district. We ventured ninety miles to SW Washington, where jobs in the lumber industry and construction field were said to be plentiful. Ninety miles felt like a world away.

Until we could find housing, we stayed with friends who were kind enough to let us stay in their spare bedroom. We arrived with only the bare necessities and what we could fit in Bill's truck and our little orange VW Beetle. We lived frugally, working hard not to dip in to what meager savings we had. The *Lesson of the Ring* phrase of "true need vs. want" phrase constantly echoed in our heads. We fastidiously searched for jobs and a roof to cover our heads. After pounding the pavement and combing every classified ad for three weeks, we finally found a very small, 500 square foot home to rent.

I accepted a part-time OT job in home health, while Bill's diversified talents landed him a job at a gasket firm catering to the lumber industry. Thankfully, our work hours and days were flexible, so the financial burden of daycare wasn't an issue.

Being new to the area, we weren't aware of all the amenities and services surrounding our little neighborhood. We knew we lived across from the county fairgrounds, but we had *no* idea how often and what events were held there—everything from odoriferous livestock shows to noisy motor sports. To say it was a quiet, pleasant smelling place was a misnomer.

Then, there was the county jail several blocks away. Our youthful ignorance and trusting the neighborhood was safe was soon tested. A worn path through our backyard blackberry patch should have given us a hint.

Capitalizing on our naivety, a locally organized group of unsavory characters began casing our little bungalow. Unbeknownst to us, the group watched our every move. We later learned this group of delinquents had been planning to spring their fearless leader, who was currently being housed in the jail for committing several felony crimes. The path through our berry patch had been part of the escape plan.

One morning before I had to be to work, I was having coffee at our friend's house—the ones we'd stayed with before we found out little abode. I went to get something out of my bag, and realized I had left some needed paperwork at home. Our friend graciously offered to watch our seven-month-old, while I hurried home to retrieve the paperwork. Five minutes later, I arrived at our bungalow. I drove up the driveway and parked the car in the carport attached to the little house.

I was not prepared for what I found. My first reaction was panic. Fear was not far behind. I discovered the main door frame splintered, the door lying askew, and swinging on one hinge. Against my better judgment, I ventured inside. What I saw was horrific. Our tiny house was trashed. Clothes were strewn everywhere and what little we owned was not in their proper places.

I promptly called the police and then Bill. Bill arrived first, with the police not far behind. The officers secured the house and did a full search to assure us no other culprits were in hiding. While the police did their work, Bill enveloped me in his arms. He held me tight, valiantly trying to get my body to quit its violent shaking. After an hour or so, the police said we could go into the house. They asked us to make an inventory of what we found missing—for the police report as well as for our insurance company. Bill and I were grateful we took our parent's advice to get renters insurance as soon as we moved in. Life lesson learned.

We were devastated when we discovered Bill's beloved, antique, Hamilton Railroad watch, given to him by my grandfather on our wedding day and his 1972 high school class ring with his initials engraved on the inside were missing. Me? I lost a whopping five dollars' worth of inexpensive costume jewelry. While my loss was *far* from Bill losses, I still felt violated.

The robbery and jail break was big news. The case was high profile, with many months of unsolved robberies attributed to these unsavory characters. It didn't take long after the break-in at our home for the police to apprehend the scoundrels, much to the justice system's (and the community's) delight.

The break in the case came when one of the delinquents attempted to pawn Bill's high school class ring. The owner of the local pawn shop had been alerted by the police of items stolen in the various robberies and knew what to be looking for. Thankfully, he was astute and paid close attention.

There it was again—God in the details—right down to engraved initials and a graduation date on a class ring. It was an outward and visual reminder God was with us. We were learning how to believe God through our doubts—in taking our first steps of faith into unfamiliar territory away from our cocoon of safety and all things familiar. With God at the helm, we courageously faced fear in the face when delinquents robbed our home and peace of mind.

As one person after another heard how the robbery ring was broken up and the delinquents apprehended, people shook their heads in disbelief. They offered their praise and thanks we were unharmed. Bill and I had a good chuckle together, especially about Bill's ring. Laughter was just the right medicine to help us heal through this traumatic ordeal and lighten our burdened hearts. A high school class ring broke up a robbery ring – go figure!

We lifted up our praise for God's providence and protection and found joy and laughter as we journeyed down new paths. Faithful friends—walking beside us as we faced life's daily battles—bolstered our faith, courage, and strength. Our friends reminded us again there *is* victory, especially when we let God lead the way.

12

DEBT IS A FOUR-LETTER WORD

As I stated earlier, foul language and unwise actions were forbidden growing up. Four years into our married life, we added our own word to the Four-Letter-List. The word consumed us for many years: D-E-B-T.

We continued renting the little bungalow for several months after the break-in. Finally, I could no longer stand it. I had the heebie-jeebies about the house and the neighborhood. I desperately pleaded to God in prayer to make a way for us to find somewhere else to live. Knowing *all* things are possible with God, I asked Him for what *I* thought was the *impossible*: to find a place we could actually afford to *buy*.

Following several years of economic downfall, the state and local economy slowly stared to rebound. The real estate market followed the upward trend of the economy. In my daily prayers, (like I needed to remind Him?) I plead and held onto Matthew19:26.

We stood steadfast on God's reminder of "possible." Every Sunday after church, we stopped by the local grocery store and picked up the Sunday paper. At home, we eagerly combed the newspaper's real estate sections.

I must tell you, there was a *slight* difference of opinions of what we thought God meant by "*all* things are possible" as we perused the Sunday paper. I was looking for a ready-to-move-in type of house—what they term *turn-key* nowadays. Bill on the other hand, ever the carpenter and DIY'er, was open to a home in needing a little of his TLC.

Bill's opinion won. He has an amazing way of looking at things—not as they necessarily are, but what they can become. He has an equally amazing way of convincing *me* to trust him, and even though *I* couldn't see the potential, he *promised* amazing results in the end.

He found a place with five acres, within our price range. We were eligible to make an offer with our pre-approved credit. The drive to the property was a scenic jaunt that passed a meandering river and forests on either side of the freeway.

Our offer and then their counter-offer were finally accepted.

Our first home purchase…let's just say *I* wasn't necessarily calling it a home—in fact, I didn't even call it a house—at least not in the condition it was in.

The building was partially framed-in. It had one bedroom, one bathroom, and an upstairs storage loft. Not a single door or window had been hung. The storage loft had been converted into what the sellers called a *potential* office or master bedroom. Both Bill and I had to duck our heads where a queen size bed might be able to fit.

Since the building was not approved to live in yet by the local county building codes, the previous occupants lived in—and left us—a well-worn, single-wide trailer placed near the semi-framed "house." Our double-sized bed filled the *entire* (and only) bedroom. We had to crawl from the foot of the bed to the head, to be able to get into bed each night. The crib snugly fit into the pantry area. Our one worldly possession, a small love-seat, and a high chair filled what remained of the living space. Heaven help us if guests popped in to visit!

Signing the real estate papers, we knew full-well this place was a labor of love. It was a true "fixer-upper." But it was ours. What we *didn't* know, nor could we ever imagine, in one short week after our very first plunge into debt, our house and property would be placed smack dab in the Red Zone of Mount St. Helens after she blew her stack, spewing ash.

God was right. All things are possible. Even when they don't happen in the way we think they should. We had many lessons to learn about not just believing in God, but point blank believing Him. We found victory, despite the challenges that came our way even when we added the word "debt" to the Four Letter List.

God was with us every step of the way.

13

FROM BEAUTY TO ASHES AND BACK AGAIN

It seemed everywhere we went, we saw someone wearing a shirt with the question, "Where were you on May 18, 1980?"

May 16th, 1980, we officially closed on our fixer-upper. Our phone line was installed late on Saturday, May 17th. On the docket for Sunday, May18th were church and a youth group pool party we were helping to chaperone. After we got home, we had planned to do a phone-a-thon to family family and friends, giving them our new phone number.

We made only *one* telephone call on the 17th—to Bill's folks, as they were going to stop in and see us on their way to visit Bill's sister in Nevada. We needed to give them directions to our cozy new digs.

There was only one problem. Excitement had so filled us— about our house *and* their visit—we forgot to give them our tele- phone number in case they got lost!

"Oh well," Bill said. "We can give it to them when they get here." (Remember, this was long before the days of cell phones and Siri in your car.)

Sunday, May 18, 1980 was a beautiful, sunny, picture-perfect Sunday.

Swimsuits, towels, life-vest for our daughter, Bibles, and finger foods for the party were packed. We were off! We took two cars to church so Bill could slip out of the youth pool party a bit early to meet his folks. We couldn't wait to share our first home and future plans with Mom and Dad.

On our way to church, just down the road from our house, there was a perfect spot to pull over and view Mount St. Helens. The mountain had been in the news of late for its recent seismic activity. I signaled to Bill, who was driving behind me, to stop.

The mountain was gorgeous—fully adorned in snow, with a small plume of seismic steam escaping out of its top. The sun shone brightly, its early morning rays reflecting on the northern slopes. We snapped a couple of post-card photos, as was our routine, to chronicle the mountain's activities. We kissed each other good-bye and off on our separate ways to church we went.

Bill headed for the freeway, but I stopped for gas at a small country store that doubled as a diner, local hang-out, and gossip center. As I was pumping gas, I watched two, then four, and then six emergency vehicles pass.

"Oh, Harry Truman and the Red Zone locals are probably stirring up a ruckus," I mused. They too, had been making the news. Every time the mountain 'burped' ash, they stood in solidarity, refusing to obey law enforcement's orders to evacuate the area for safety measures.

I went inside to pay for my gas.

"Anyone know what the commotion is?" I asked.

"Nope, nothing here—not even on the C.B. radio," the clerk replied.

The locals sitting at the breakfast bar shook their heads as well.

I headed back to my little, orange VW bug. Once on the road, I drove the twenty minutes south on the freeway, where our church was located.

When I arrived at church, Bill was waiting for me at the fellowship hall door. We made our way to the sanctuary and took our seats. After receiving communion, church deacons approached us. We were peppered with questions and wild-eyed concern. I stared blankly back at them. I didn't have a clue what they were talking about.

"Did you see it on your way down the aisle?"

"Mount St. Helens blew!"

"Say what?" I voiced my shock.

"Mount St. Helens blew!!" Someone shouted.

Radios could be heard from the back pew as the deacons monitored the news closely.

I turned my head to look through a large, plate-glass window. In horror, I saw gigantic, black and gray plumes, spewing higher and higher, heading upward and then east. It was *not* the serene mountain we had taken photos of an hour ago.

Bill and I didn't know whether to stay or leave. In our mid-twenties, with an almost one-year old, our thoughts were muddled. Oh, how we wished we knew where on the road Mom and Dad were. They always knew what to do. No matter what a situation was, they knew what to say and how best to direct us. But we were on our own. We knew we had to trust the One who is our very help in times of trouble.

We decided the best thing we could do was to stay right where we were. The freeways and many of the roads we had just driven were now closed. Some of the roads were placed in the Red Zone, along with our house (or half-house) of not even a week. It was now possibly in harm's way. A volcano blowing was new for everyone. The panic in radio announcers' voices was evident.

I fidgeted as the morning's Scripture was read. I couldn't believe my ears. *This* was the passage chosen for this morning?

> *God is our refuge and strength,*
> *an ever-present help in trouble.*
> *Therefore we will not fear, though the earth gives way*
> *and the mountains fall into the heart of the sea,*

Though its waters roar and foam,
and the mountains quake with their surging.
– Psalm 46 NLB

In the middle of the church service, Bill was fidgety. He finally laid a hand on my knee and said, "I've got to go." His whispered words conveyed all I needed to know. I knew it was incredibly hard for him to sit still and do nothing while the mountain continued to erupt. Our home was possibly in danger. Added to the tension we were feeling, we had no idea where his parents were.

His words to me were firm. "Stay here. I have to see if I can get home, just in case Mom and Dad make it. Plus, I need to know if our place is still standing, check on the animals, get water barrels filled if I can and check the electricity. After church, you go to the pool party. I will call you when I can." He kissed our daughter and gave me a long kiss, doing his best to reassure me God was watching over all of us.

I numbly nodded my head. Bill was my all in all. I counted on him to know what to do and where to go for the three of us. Bill knew our best safety measure was for our daughter and me to be at the home of the pool party. Luckily for us, the wind was blowing the ash away from where we lived and toward Eastern Washington. Even so, our house was only twelve miles from the now volatile and erupting volcano. At the home of the pool party I could watch the news reports and hear the latest up-to-date information. I had to trust Bill. I had to trust God. I was not alone. I kept whispering to myself, "God is my refuge and strength—an ever-present help in trouble." I *had* to trust.

True to His Word, God was our refuge and strength. Bill made it home and our house was safe. He was able to get one phone call out to me before all the lines went dead.

14

BREAKER, BREAKER – YOU GOT A COPY?

Meanwhile, Bill's parents were on the road to our place. They were caught in the maze and mayhem of detours due to the eruption. Providentially, Dad was a trucker and knew many back roads. He was also an assistant volunteer fire chief, so he was able to tap into emergency CB radio lines. Try as many back roads as they could, they were able to get close, but not close enough. They told us later somehow, Mom convinced a state trooper through her tears they *had* to be let through the closed road to get to their son's house.

By the grace of God, the trooper knew who we were. He told them of an unknown back road Dad could take—but they had to hurry as he had orders to close the road in five minutes. The trooper quickly gave them directions to our new place. Bill was doing one final safety check on our so-far-safe home, when Mom and Dad drove up our dirt driveway.

I sat glued to the television along with many at the youth event. News anchors reported all telephone communications in the region were down. I tried not to panic. I so wanted to be with Bill. If something were to happen, I wanted the three of us to be together, not separated.

Just then, I heard the owner of the home talking on a CB radio. He happened to be the mayor of the town. He was monitoring the radio waves and communicating with officials via the CB.

Knowing Bill's dad and his prolific use of a CB as a truck driver, I asked the mayor if I could use his CB to try to reach Bill's folks. After much pleading and reassuring him I knew how to use it, he relented.

I pushed the call button, praying for a miracle. Using Dad's CB handle (name) and my own CB handle, I spoke into the microphone, "Breaker, Breaker, Dairy Bill this is Strump-pot"—the Dutch nickname Bill's dad called me—"You got a copy?"

The lines crackled and then they went silent.

I tried again. "Breaker, Breaker, Dairy Bill, this is Strump-pot. You got a copy?" I released the button and waited for what seemed an eternity.

This time a faint voice could be heard.

"Breaker, Breaker, this is Dairy Bill, Strump-pot, is that you? What's your twenty?" (CB lingo for "where are you?")

Tears streaming down my cheeks as I heard Dad's voice, I replied, "Copy Dairy Bill! I'm still at the pool party. Over ?"

"Copy that Strump-pot. The State Patrol is giving you clearance to come home. They have your license number and what kind of car you are driving. Leave *NOW*! The troopers are giving you fifteen minutes to get onto the interstate heading north. After that, all roads and the freeway in both directions will be barricaded closed. Your house and road are now part of the Red Zone. Troopers will be looking for you—they have a Bear in the Air who will be watching for you and over you. Over?"

My eyes continued to well up with tears. Knowing a State Patrolman in a helicopter was watching out for me, flying overhead, filled my heart fill with relief. "10-4, Dairy Bill—I'm on my way with Little Package (Jamie's handle) Strump-pot—over and out!" I hurriedly grabbed our essentials and rapidly headed to the interstate.

My little, orange VW Beetle, was the *only* vehicle on the interstate. My hands gripped the steering wheel so tight my knuckles turned white. As my little package and I putt-putted along, we slowly made our way toward home. At one point, I looked out my left window. The indelible scene of the immense flow of logs floating down the river astounded me. I kept telling myself to breathe. Later on, we'd see my little orange "Herbie", a mere speck next to the unforgettable log flow, featured on all the television news channels, taken from the State Troopers' helicopter footage. It was overwhelming.

One more battle, one more obstacle, one more adventure, and lesson in faith and courage!

Mom and Dad stayed for an extra day, not leaving until making sure they could get access to roads allowing them to continue south to visit Bill's sister in Nevada. They promised to return in time to celebrate our daughter's first birthday, the following week.

With parts of the freeway and many roads closed, and our house now in the Red Zone, we had to carry our real estate papers with us at all times, plus picture identification. The papers allowed us to get in and out of closed roads and proved we honestly *did* live in the Red Zone area, since our new driver's licenses with our new address had not arrived yet. It was our only way to get to the grocery store, stock up on supplies, and get back home.

We tied a knot on the rope of unknowns and held on tight. Not just to the rope, but to God's promises He was with us, no matter what. He daily showed us the truth of His Word. He was and *is* our refuge and very present help in times of trouble.

15

ROUND TWO

True to their word, Mom and Dad arrived back in time to watch our daughter blow her first birthday candle out. We grinned as she grabbed a fistful of chocolate frosting with a teensy bit of lemon cake and stuffed it in her mouth. She laughed with glee as she grabbed another fistful of frosting and clapped her chocolate covered hands together, then proceeded to smear it all over her face as well as her high-chair table top. She looked at us with a look conveying "Isn't this what I was supposed to do?"

With all of the excitement from the mountain's eruption, the long trip to Nevada and back, and participating in our one-year-old's first birthday antics, Bill's folks told us they were going to turn in early, retiring to their trailer. As dad walked out, he chuckled as he said to Bill, "I'll be sure to come wake you up at my regular get-up time!"

Bill replied, "You wake me up before six and you'll be sorry!" They both laughed. We headed to bed shortly after.

The next morning we awoke to a *pound-pound-pound* sound on our trailer door. It was pitch black outside. Bill groaned, "So help me, if this is dad's idea of a joke, he's got another think coming," as he ambled out of bed. He glanced at the wall clock as he headed for the door.

"*Seven o'clock? That's weird. It should be light by now,*" he thought to himself.

The pounding on the door intensified.

"Hurry up, will ya?" By now, Dad was yelling loudly. "The mountain erupted again and ash is coming down hard!"

Bill quickly opened the door. It looked like it was snowing, but it was gray, not white. And it was the month of May.

Two gray figures emerged from the concrete flurry of ash falling from the sky.

I donned my robe and joined them in the living area. The power was out. I looked outside. "It looks like the gooey oobleck from the Dr. Seuss book *Bartholomew and the Oobleck*." I stated.

Dad replied, "It's not gooey. It's pure grit."

Aftershock earthquakes from the second eruption came at regular intervals, rattling the 1950's trailer, and our nerves as well. More than once we leaned against a wall to regain our balance.

After helping Mom and Dad out of their ash-covered coats, we looked at each other with the discernable question… now what?

All five of us were in unfamiliar territory, but we knew we weren't alone. We could feel God's peace settle over us.

"First off, let's get some light on in here," Bill said grabbed his battery operated camping lantern. Our trailer was small enough the one lantern was sufficient. Luckily, we had a propane tank for heat, so we were warm and could use the kitchen stove. Bill also had a generator he often used on jobs—it was needed to save our refrigerated and frozen food.

Mom and I let Bill and his dad come up with a plan. First, they checked the breaker boxes and got the things covered that might be in harm's way from the unknown substance continuing to fall from the sky. Next, they checked the animals. We had twenty chickens, three pygmy goats, and five pigs. They locked them in their pens, making sure their food and water were not contaminated, and they were safely sheltered.

The vehicles were next. A former dairy farmer, Dad now drove a milk-tanker truck for Darigold Farms™ so he always carried extra milk filters. He told Bill our vehicles needed to be protected from the ash when we drove them, and to use the milk filters as an extra air filter. As time and the ash wore on, we were more than grateful for Dad's smart, practical, thinking. His advice saved our car engines from getting ruined, unlike many friends' vehicles, where the ash clogged and caused havoc, not to mention costly damage.

We tuned the radio to get the latest emergency information. With this second eruption, the wind was blowing due West-Southwest. We were in the direct path of the ash-fall. The wind direction was totally opposite of the previous week's eruption that had coated Eastern Washington and parts farther East with the grit. By early afternoon, the sky lightened and ash fall fell slower. Gleaning information from the news, Bill's parents felt they had only a small window of opportunity to head north and back home to Enumclaw.

We chose to stay, protecting our property. But this time, Mom and Dad had our telephone number—just "in case."

We said our long and tearful good-byes, hugging them a bit tighter than usual. While our family had always lived with the Scripture verses found in Matthew 6:33-34—living life one day at a time; not worrying about tomorrow as it had enough cares of its own, it took on a whole new meaning. We *literally* had no idea what the morrow might bring, much less how we were going to navigate through these uncharted times.

Maybe you have had 'eruptions' in your life, where you literally had no idea what the morrow will bring, much less how you were going to navigate through uncharted situations. These are the times when turning the helm over to God and let *Him* steer, is the best option and decision—and a true way to find peace in the midst of the storm.

16

WHEN THE ASH SETTLED

In the weeks and months following the eruptions of Mount St. Helens, uncertainty hung heavy over the entire region. Not only had lives been lost in the eruption—including Harry Truman's—but the land for miles was devastated.

The landscape looked eerie. In places it resembled pictures of the first moon landing. We had to wear protective masks to prevent inhaling the lingering ash particles—especially when the wind blew. Homes were lost and acres of pristine woodlands were leveled.

The only up-side was the volcanic ash coated everything, making the gardens in the area prolific for summers to come!

This area of SW Washington was economically dependent upon the logging industry in all forms. Jobs vaporized as quickly as the forest did when the mountain erupted. Large lumber and shipping corporations took huge hits. Cargo ships could no longer make it up the mighty Columbia River to unload its cargo– even ports as far away as Portland, Oregon. The river was clogged with the downed trees and mounds of ash and mud. Until a plan to deal with the vast unknowns could be made, jobs in all sectors came to a standstill. Both directions of the freeway and many roads continued to be closed.

Unemployment in our area had had been declining, increased dramatically after the eruption. The trickle effect hit the counties and the regions nearby. The logging industry wasn't the only in-dustry that had been hit hard. The vast number of industries asso-ciated with logging and dependent upon the industry—much like shirt-tail relatives, got hit too. Mill workers, gasket companies, shipping, equipment companies, the petroleum industry, jobs re-lated to the many ports, the longshoremen… *all* were in limbo. As uncertainty grew, more economic areas were affected, including grocery stores and schools. Families moved away as daily supplies and jobs became scarce.

We were not to escape the economic calamity. The gasket company Bill had been working for catered to the logging and shipping industries. Corporate Headquarters in New York decid-ed to close the area office where Bill worked, to cut their losses from the aftermath of Mount St. Helens erupting. He was offered a position in New York State, but declined. Turning a city girl into a country girl is one thing. But taking a farm boy away from any semblance of a rural area could not be reconciled. So Bill became one more employment casualty, relegated to the unemployment line and an uncertain future.

Just like I described in the preface, Bill felt like the worn out t-shirt. He felt tattered, torn, and full of holes. Bill felt less than whole. He felt useless. How will he provide for his family? There were *no* jobs in the areas he was skilled. The saving grace was *my* job was still safe—even though it was only part-time.

We decided his best option was staying home and finishing our first home. Luckily, we had already purchased the needed building supplies before the mountain erupted. Bill's staying at home, as a house-husband was still unconventional at the time. But that didn't bother him! He enjoyed being in charge of making meals, shopping, and caring for our daughter, all while he finished building the house. It was tight financially. *Very* tight. To this day, I'm not sure if Bill or I will *ever* purposely eat ramen noodles for a meal.

We were blessed when a full-time, local occupational therapy job was offered to me via my network of OT colleagues. The job led me from being a home health OT and allowed me to expand and gain experience in the mental health aspect of occupation therapy. I knew learning skills in an area I was not particularly gifted in, nor proficient at, and offer me a chance to further expand my professional repertoire. Who knew what future career advancement and opportunities might present themselves in the years ahead? Plus, we could sorely use the extra income a full-time job with benefits offered.

At an Adult Day Treatment Center, I worked doing individual counseling, small group therapy, and taught Daily Living Skills classes for adults transitioning from in-patient mental health facilities back into the community. I was stretched in ways I never could have imagined with my new job.

Mental health issues were so under-addressed—and still are—and the needs of the people were, at times, overwhelming. Working in this environment made me cling to my faith in God tighter than ever. With many clients, the issues they struggled with made danger ever-present. I was grateful for the heavenly hedge of protection I knew was around me.

Within days of accepting the Adult Day Treatment job, I was also offered an early morning part-time job at the local YMCA. My skills set fit the bill to be the Director of their Swim Rehabilitation program to a "T". I was an occupational therapist, I had been a competitive swimmer in high school, and in college I took courses allowing me to become credentialed to teach swim classes, water safety courses, and gain my swim team coaching qualifications.

I *love* swimming. The Swim Rehab job was a fun job. While every dollar earned helped our bleeding budget immensely, it was hard to believe I was being paid to keep in shape *and* keep my OT continuing education hours current! I was blessed to be able to combine my love for swimming and my passion for OT.

What a delight and thrill it was for me to help people. Once they were immersed in the warm pool water where gravity was eliminated, it became possible for them to exercise paralyzed or impaired limbs. It was sheer joy to see them smile and to watch their reaction of elation, wonder and amazement as they discovered they could actually move their limbs with ease and much less pain. It was a win-win for all.

So… three, very-early-mornings a week, I groggily rolled out of bed, grabbed my swim gear bag and work clothes, and headed out the door by 5:30 a.m. Thank goodness for hoodies and sweatpants to pull on! By the time I finished making the twenty-minute commute to the Y, I was mostly awake. Before jumping into the pool, I took the health department's mandated shower—which was always quite cold early in the morning. The cold shower jolted me to complete alertness!

Two hours always flew by quickly. Promptly at 8:00 a.m., I hustled out of the pool to get ready for my 'real' job. After a quick *warm* shower, I got dressed, chugged down a quick mocha, and made the short five-minute commute to get to work on time by 9:00 a.m. Funny how I always seemed to be refreshed and in a better mood on the days I had been at the pool!

Back at home, Bill was equally busy. Leave it to my creative husband who relied on his farming skills, baling-wire tactics, and bare bones budgeting to help us make ends meet. With our animals, the price of feed was tough on our lean budget. One morning, while trying to figure out a solution—besides selling the animals—a light bulb went on for Bill.

He decided to go around to several grocery stores and talk to the produce and bakery managers, asking them what they did with the outdated product or items that couldn't be put out. Their reply was they just threw it in the dumpster. He immediately offered to come and take it off their hands and even offered to help them collect, carry, and pack the boxes of items. The managers were elated. We were *ecstatic*!

Once Bill got the bakery and produce boxes home each day, he sorted through everything. We couldn't believe what had to be thrown out by industry standards and regulations.

Bill placed the items into two categories: feed for the animals, and manna from Heaven for us. We ate like royalty! Many of the items thrown out were still in very edible shape. On our tight budget, there were often items we'd *never* been able to afford before delicacies like fresh pineapple, mushrooms, and mangos - even Artisan breads graced our dinner table. Occasionally there were even chocolate covered donuts with sprinkles and powdered sugar coated donut holes, much to Bill and our daughter's delight. I was blessed on the days they saved me at least *one* donut hole.

Bill became beloved at the stores. His "at the end of his hand" demeanor of encouragement, help, and joy were contagious. So much so, occasionally the butcher or dairy manager slipped something into Bill's truck, unbeknownst to him. When Bill discovered the items once he arrived home, it was a day to rejoice indeed. One day, the butcher stealthily slipped a prime rib in the truck. We couldn't believe it! God was more than true to His word, providing for our *every* need (and more!) Worry was *not* to be in our vocabulary, as long as we turned the helm over to Him.

Between grocery runs, finishing the house, getting the garden going, regular house chores of laundry, dusting, vacuuming, *plus* potty-training a toddler, Bill hardly had time to be bored.

He went through *three* vacuum cleaners as he tried to clean up after the second Mount St. Helens eruption. Even with extra air filters, Bill discovered the grit of the volcanic ash was "the gift that kept on giving." Just when he thought he had cleaned it all up, a windy day blew through stirring up hidden pockets of ash all over again.

I chuckled (when I knew it might fall on receptive ears) and say, "Huh! Not so easy being the one staying at home, is it?"

Jokingly, he scowled, and gave me one of "those" looks.

We found hitting life head-on was not always easy. Nor were the times when we experienced the "poorer" and "worse" parts of our wedding vows. It took dedicated, *deliberate* and intentional work on both of our parts to keep communication lines open, to encourage each other, and show each other respect. Our marriage was about team-work and commitment, trusting each other and above all else, trusting God for our every need. One day at a time.

How is your team-work going as you face your daily battles?

17

OUR SUMMER SURPRISE

Mid-summer into Bill's second year of staying at home, we received a phone call from a teen-aged girl I used to baby-sit back when *I* was a teenager. Over the years her parents had been strong footsteps in the sands of time for me. I shared their story in *Loose Screws and Skinned Knees*. They had helped me through some of my toughest times as a teenager. Now, on the other end of the phone line, their soon-to-be junior in high school was asking, no *pleading*, for our help.

Jenne was a very bright, musically and academically gifted, somewhat shy, gentle soul. She was also a typical teen, who, at the age of sixteen, had the ingredients and actions necessary for a perfect parental storm. Her age, adolescent attitude, hormones, her desperate efforts to attempt be an adult, all melded to produce what her parents later described to us as an "F-5 Teen-Tornado." It was hard for me to imagine *any* of these traits and undertakings. Then again, I had not been around her in her recent years.

In Jenne's typical teen mindset, parents knew nothing and were clueless to the current generation's vast superior intelligence. Any parental opinion directed toward Jenne was therefore rendered null and void. Any parental *request* of said teen were be met with eyes rolling upward, a heavy sigh heaved, and feet loudly stomping as she descended the stairs to her bedroom. Jenne proceeded to lock her bedroom door and purposely turn the music up so loud her "unreasonable, irrational and difficult parents"—her words—could not invade her private space. She longed to spend her summer *anywhere* but where her difficult-to-deal-with parents were *not.*

Hence, the reasons for her telephone call to us.

Jenne asked if she could spend four to six weeks with us. She used the pretense she could help us by babysitting and doing household chores, allowing Bill to focus fully on finishing up the house. She told us she didn't want any pay—just the chance to have a change of scenery and get a breather from her parents.

After talking with her mom and dad, we agreed to take the teen on. Truthfully, letting Jenne come stay with us was an answer to prayer for all involved. Jenne's parents could use the time-out from teen tirades. Bill could use an extra set of hands as he put the finishing touches on the house. Many of the tasks were difficult to accomplish with a toddler under foot. And, I could relax and not always feel like I had to rush home to relieve Bill.

Jenne had the opportunity to experience an entirely different lifestyle than her extremely successful, architect father provided. She also had time, away from her family and friends, to think about her future. Post high school graduation decisions were heavy on her mind.

The Jenne we saw was more like the girl we were used to—but occasionally, when certain topics or buttons were pushed, or hormones were at their height, we could get a glimpse of what Jenne's parents dealt with on a full-time basis. No wonder they could all use some time-out. All in all, it was a great month and a half.

Jenne cared for Jamie as Bill continued alternating his days hanging cedar-siding on the exterior of the house, landscaping, and keeping up with the *huge* Dutch garden he had put in. Row after row of gladiolus, dahlias, peas, kohlrabi, carrots, lettuce, potatoes, cabbage, and more could be seen from our front windows. On the weekends, he shifted gears and worked on building a playhouse—complete with swings, a slide, and cedar-siding to match the house.

Having Jenne around especially helped when an occasional, paid, odd job for Bill came up. He helped move equipment into the Red Zone to start the restoration process and the re-building roads. Church members called him, asking to hire him to help with short term projects. The change of pace and scenery were a welcome change from working on the house. It was an enormous relief we didn't have to worry about child-care expenses and we knew Jamie was in capable hands.

Alas, Jenne's time flew by. Soon it was Labor Day, and time for her to return home. We had been praying about what we to do for day-care, once Jenne had to leave. It wasn't an easy situation when we lived out in the country on a tight budget. As a mom, I tried not to worry, and leave it in God's Good Hands. True to His Word, when we let go and let God, prayers were answered.

The weekend after Jenne left, our neighbor came over to let us know she was starting a day-care. She said she greatly appreciated it if we could pass the word along to anyone we knew in need of help for their children. We could never imagine God's provision in our time of need coming from right next door and willing to barter fresh eggs for day-care fees?

*God*incidence!

18

HUMILITY AND THE HOUSE-HUSBAND

Even with my job(s) and the extra odd work Bill did, finances continued to be tight. We hadn't exactly budgeted for the after-math of an erupting volcano to enter and impact our financial picture. The burden began to take an emotional toll on Bill. He took his role as head of the house seriously. *He* wanted to be the financial provider. He didn't like the fact I was working two jobs, often requiring long hours. Not having steady full-time work was discouraging to him. He was getting desperate and then finally broke. He didn't care *what* the job was, or what it paid, he *needed* to work.

The only job available at the time was a tree planter, replanting trees in the blow-down area around Mount St. Helens. It paid a whopping four dollars an hour, plus a small, token commission for each tree planted. It was a job few working-class men considered, even when times were tough, but Bill humbly set his pride aside and took the job.

He felt a sense of renewal. He was back to working full-time. It elated him to be out in the great outdoors—even with the endless days of damp, chill-to-the-bone Pacific Northwest rain. Very few of the men on his crew spoke English, and many were a band of drug-using unsavory type characters – using even on the job. After our previous encounter with unsavory characters, he didn't let anyone know where we lived.

Tree planter's hours were notoriously long. Six days a week, Bill met the work van and his co-laborers at four in the morning at a local parking lot. Thankfully it was only ten minutes from our house. Then around seven or eight o'clock in the evening, he arrived home, weary and worn.

Planting the tree seedlings required climbing up and down over uneven, rugged, often steep terrain. The crew daily tromped through leftover ash sometimes up to a foot deep before digging the holes to plant the tree seedlings. When Bill started to get weary, he "re-booted" his attitude and belted out some of his favorite worship songs. As his voice carried over the hills and valleys, it brought smiles to his co-workers as they worked. The non-English-speaking men may not have understood all of the words Bill boomed out, but they recognized "Jesus" as the subject of the songs.

If discouragement started to set in, Bill countered negative thoughts by replacing them with the knowledge one day he could point to the growing trees and say, "I helped replant that forest!" He refused to let the enemy get a foothold and deter him.

After many months of the back-breaking, low-paying, hard labor, Bill hit bottom. One morning, as I blearily woke up to my internal "make-sure-Bill-got-off-to-work alarm clock," I realized it was four-thirty. Bill should have been long gone. Instead, he was snoring like a hibernating bear.

Seconds later, I heard a vehicle drive up our driveway. I was petrified. I vigorously shook Bill awake. He pulled his jeans on and bumbled down the stairs.

He was greeted with loud cheers in a language that was *not* English. Were they urging him to hurry up? I was too afraid to even look out the window. I had heard tales of some of the men's capers, and I didn't want to put faces to the stories. How did they even know where we lived? Thoughts barreled in of our former house break-in. I tried to push them away.

As Bill came back inside, I assumed he'd he grab the rest of his gear and the lunch I had made him the night before. Instead, he lumbered up the stairs and collapsed on the bed.

"I just quit," he managed to blurt out before he was snoring again.

I wasn't able to sleep so I silently prayed: "*Thank You, God for protecting us these last few months. I have no idea how Bill's crew found our place, but I am more than grateful for the hedge of protection placed around us. I promise to trust You, as You know where we're headed from here—I know we sure don't.*"

I rolled over, snuggled under the still warm covers and cuddled up to my best friend.

Bill was glad to be a full-time house-husband again. He was glad to pick up his familiar tool-belt and get back to the home-stretch of finishing the house. As he put up the final pieces of the cedar on the outside of the house he had another ah-ha moment. Once the outside was completely finished and sealed, he turned his attention to putting the left-over cedar siding on the interior walls. Oh, it smelled *sooo* good!

At long last, but by far not the least, Bill laid the carpet. We enjoyed walking barefoot, sinking our toes in the shag. We sat on the floor more than we did our couch! No more particle board slivers in our feet! I don't think a day passed without a comment—or two or three!—about how we thoroughly enjoyed having the luxury of carpet. Sometimes the little things are actually quite *big*.

Barely a month after we laid the carpet, I received a totally un-expected OT job offer in another community. It was an incredible opportunity.

The decision did not come easy. We were so proud of our first home. We loved where we lived and had grown close to many in the community—especially after Mount St. Helens blew. What about the Swim Rehab Program? Could they find someone qualified to look after it and my special needs buddies? Sigh...a choice had to be made.

We spent hours praying, talking, bantering back and forth. We made a list of pros vs. cons. In our hearts we *knew* we could not afford to pass the offer up. The financial and benefit package offered was more than we *ever* dreamed. It was our pride holding us back from making a decision. We were proud of our accomplishments. Finishing the house, living through the eruption and aftermath of Mount St. Helens, our growth and maturity in jobs we loved.

Common sense and a settling peace made the final decision. I accepted the job.

We didn't know it at the time, but this was to be the first of many times putting carpet down was our signature warning of, "Get ready. You're about to move!

It was also an introduction to another, greater lesson: The four-letter-word *debt* can be overwhelming, burdensome, and taxing. It can even bring on double trouble.

19

DOUBLE DEBT

The carpet had been laid. The job offer had been accepted. My new job would involve developing a new occupational therapy program, in a town about thirty miles north of our DIY- turned key-turn home.

What *hadn't* occurred to us was our first home, ready for someone to move in, didn't sell right away. Deep in the caverns of our heart we knew God had the perfect buyer in mind; we just didn't know when.

In the meantime, we did what many not-financially savvy young couples do. We used the collateral of our first home to get a pre-approved second mortgage loan. We couldn't rationalize the gas money, the wear and tear on our vehicles, nor did the extra time spend commuting to my new job. We were determined to keep our tenets of faith and family first. Time together was precious, and the commute was cutting into that time.

Until we found a home we could afford, people from our new church home stepped up. They offered to let us stay at various church members' homes, often trading rent for odd jobs and repairs they needed done. Realtors who attended the church the church helped us find month-to-month rentals or long-term house-sitting when they had houses on the market that weren't moving. But more times than we hoped, we had to dip into the second mortgage money to cover rent.

The job I accepted allowed us to get our feet on a wee bit more stable ground, even though we were in double-debt, holding a mortgage payment in addition to rent. Plus we still had regular household bills, medical expenses, food, and gas. There were many days our daily financial life felt overwhelming at best.

There were some days it felt like our heads were barely above the tsunami of bills we had incurred. It felt like torrents threatening to wash over and drown us. Working extra hours barely made a dent in the budget. This went on for over a year.

Each month as I paid the bills, I began with the plea, "Lord, *please* let there be enough money in our bank account." And there always was enough...until I blew it.

Before we ever said our "I do's," Bill and I had agreed the *first* check written *before* any bills were to be paid, was our tithe check to our local church. We also agreed the check written was to be a straight ten percent, no matter how big or little our paychecks were. We had been taught about tithing early in our premarital counseling. It had been a new concept to us, but it made total sense. God had more than blessed our lives. Who were we to withhold what rightfully was His and what He had blessed us with? And, it was a clear instruction from the Bible.

Then it happened. I fell into the temptation Bill and I said we should try to avoid at *all* costs. We felt confident we could avoid the pitfall.

Go figure, it was me, not Bill, who was lured into the trap of not giving to God first. The guilt of failure weighed heavy on me. The *only* time we were *ever* delinquent on bills were the months I didn't pay our tithe first, or withheld it altogether. I figured we could use the extra to help us get by. I justified it was only for a short time - only until we were out of our double-debt situation.

Fortunately, with some Heavenly prodding and keister-kicking, it only took me a couple months to figure out the huge error of my ways. In withholding our tithe—figuring it might ease our financial burden—did the exact opposite.

From that day to present day, I have never fallen back into the trap of not giving to God what was His. We've never been delinquent on any financial obligation since. There were many times over the years the provision for our finances came in the strangest of ways, but the provision was always there.

While I was still feeling the guilt and sting of failure, drowning in self-pity, I felt God's familiar hand of mercy on my shoulder, assuring me things were going to be okay and work out. I only had to trust Him and continue to do what I knew was right. It was as if a Heavenly life buoy was thrown to me.

Onward I walked, head held high. No more self-condemnation. So, why was I so surprised when I was offered an opportunity for professional development and career advancement in a new arena of occupational and physical therapy in ergonomics and workplace rehabilitation?

The innovative position offered a substantial and generous pay raise. An added bonus was my commute time could be cut to ten minutes from where we were renting. The position encompassed program development and implementation to rehabilitate injured workers and addressing ergonomics in the work place. Taking the job was a big risk on my part. But I *knew* it was God's tangible love and mercy surrounding us. It was humbling and an undeserved answer to my selfish prayers to bail us out of the mess my actions had put us in, financially. Even so, I was blown away in how God mercifully answered my self-centered prayer…with his unselfish love.

And if that wasn't affirmation enough of God's tangible love and mercy surrounding us, an offer on our first home, "the DIYer", was made on the *exact* same day I accepted the new job offer. We closed the final chapter of our first home on the very first day of my new job.

Once again a reminder God is *always* in the details.

20

FLIPPED OUT OVER A FIXER-UPPER

The owner of the office where I was the new director hired Bill to remodel what had formerly been a J.C. Penney™ store. The old brick building was originally constructed in the late 1890's. As Bill remodeled, he often discovered gems in little nooks and crannies and long forgotten storage spaces—especially in the basement.

I was elated when he discovered an oak mirror, and a buttonhook with the J.C. Penney™ name, logo, and the year 1898 imprinted on it. As an occupational therapist, I often used a plastic buttonhook when teaching adaptive dressing skills with clients. We put the antique buttonhook on display in the front bay window, where mannequins used to don the current fashions.

I knew what miracles Bill's carpentry mind and hands performed. It was amazing watching him transform a former department store into a rehabilitation center. I never tired of the fruits of his labor and his God-given gifts. Just as I had watched him transform our first house from its partially-framed work stage to a beautiful cedar-sided finished home. In the ten years we had been married, I proudly gazed at numerous results of his specialized handiwork seen in the various residential and commercial buildings he helped build, remodel, or renovate.

Knowing Bill's keen and practical eye could spot just the right place for us, I deferred the task of house-hunting for our second home to him. He spent hours looking for "just the right place" with what little free time he had—mostly on lunch-hours or weekends. My plate was *more* than full. Ergonomics and work place rehabilitation was an emerging field. It required developing informational pamphlets, publications, and educational marketing, not to mention speaking engagements… and being a wife… and a mom…and active in our church…and…you get the picture!

One day toward the end of our lunch hour, Bill came sauntering into my office. I knew he had left the building earlier, so I figured he was checking back in before the afternoon rush of clients. While yes, he was checking in, he also casually remarked he had put money down on a house he *knew* I'd love. The tone of his voice conveyed his excitement. He could barely contain himself. "Wait until you see it! I'll show it to you right after work!"

"You did *what?*! You put money down without showing me or asking me first?" My reply was no less than irate.

"Well… you *did* trust me and put me in charge of finding us a home, didn't you?" A twinkle in his chocolate-brown eyes accompanied his sheepish, sly smile and nonchalant words. He knew I couldn't resist.

What a lesson in trust I had coming!

After work, Bill drove me the four miles from my new office to our eventual new home. He explained the house was an historic, turn-of-the-century log house. It sat on ten, wooded acres, with majestic trees for our daughter to climb on and make forts in, plus the acreage had a long upward sloping hill for hours of playing hide-and-go-seek with her friends.

I knew I had to trust Bill. I had to look through *his* eyes and the possibilities of what *he* saw in this property. Over the years I had worked hard to learn from his ability to imagine the unimaginable. As I stepped out of our vehicle, I did my best to see the potential.

Bill knew I had dreamed of living in a log house someday. But even from the outside, I could tell a lot of work was needed to get *this* log house up to par. Maybe my deep love for Bill had grown such I could overlook and forget about his recycle and repurpose mindset. Or perhaps it was just faith, because in this instance for me, my *seeing* was far from *believing*.

Okay, so the cement steps leading up to the front door were slanted and crumbling…a lot. An easy fix for Mr. Concrete… eventually. Bill opened the wooden door for me. As it creaked on crooked hinges, I slowly took a tentative step inside. It wasn't so much a step filled with fear and trepidation—it was more like I had *no* idea what to expect.

"Oh look – it has concrete floors." I mustered as much cheer as I could into my voice.

My gaze darted about to take in the rest of the scene before me.

For some strange reason, the electrical box drew my attention. As I took tentative steps over to it, I drew in a sharp breath. The panel door was wide open. As I ventured closer, I saw a disturbing death had occurred there and let out a shriek. A creature had literally been shocked to its demise. I think it had been a mouse at one time—its arms and legs outstretched, mouth agape, teeth exposed, with a dangling tail. I couldn't help but shiver at the sight, but then it made me laugh. It was straight out of the cartoons we watched with our four-year-old.

Moving on from the grisly scene, I scanned the walls—if you could even call them such. The walls were paper thin—as in decades' old, complete with the date, local newspaper thin. No sheetrock, no carpet.

"How old *is* this house?" I shot the question to my hubby.

"1928!" Pride oozed from the grin on his face.

"Oh!" I attempted to keep my chin up for him, willing myself to not let tears of disappointment slip out.

Too afraid to try the stairs, I gazed upward to where Bill told me two bedrooms could be. I then took hesitant steps over to what I thought might be the kitchen. I let out a piercing, blood curdling scream. A garden snake hissed back at me, slithering up from the bowels of the rust-crusted kitchen sink drain.

"*Don't wimp out, Care, don't wimp out…*" I murmured to myself. I was *terrified* of snakes.

"Are you *serious*? Are you out of your ever-living mind?" I lashed out at Bill. I was more than angry. *Livid* was a more appropriate description.

I ran past Bill, still trembling from seeing the snake, tears streaming down my cheeks. Collapsing on the filthy, crumbling steps outside the house, I tried to compose myself. I wanted a home ready to move into, *not* another fixer-upper. I was tired of the extra work a DIY house needed.

A still small voice nudged and reminded me: *You did trust Bill to find you a house.*

But my heart didn't want to hear the voice I knew to be God's.

Do you really think Bill could put your hard-earned money down on a house if he didn't firmly believe you had faith in him, and his God-given gifts and talents?

The Holy Spirit's nudge was spot-on. I *did* trust Bill. I *did* believe in his God-given gifts and talents. They were the traits I loved. But I was weary of time-consuming, messy remodeling.

I heard Bill's footsteps as they approached me. He sat down on the crumbling steps next to me.

I choked out my apologies and collapsed in his arms.

He apologized for not fully preparing me for the current shape of the house.

Once again, we found coming to the end of ourselves, extending grace and forgiveness to each other. It was a life lesson we oft return to—all because God forgives us.

21

JESUS WITH SKIN ON

It took a good six months, but with blood, sweat equity, loads of help from our small group at church and an array of friends, the log house slowly took shape. Volunteers bravely took single-edge razor blades to painstakingly scrape off umpteen-years-old and multiple layers of paint from window panes. The paint was so thick on several windows it had fused and bonded the windows shut. There were sixteen panes per window and six windows downstairs alone. It was quite a chore.

These angels in disguise were my first introduction to what it the phrase "Jesus with skin on" meant. Our friends and loved ones created a flower bed, brought bags of garden soil, and planted fresh annuals to decorate the front of the house. Men laboriously whacked a pasture of unmown grass. Eventually the mown hay became our front lawn.

Friends – being "Jesus with skin on." What does one do without them?

Since Bill was working full time, his progress on the remodel was slow, but sure. Over time, Bill added a shop and a carport, which doubled as a covered basketball court. He designed, built, and landscaped an area for a hot tub. He also built a playhouse, nestled amongst the trees and overlooking a local valley.

This house brought (and will continue to bring back) memories lasting more than several life-times. It brought us lessons of love, forgiveness, faith, and a peace passing all understanding. Many of these lessons were hard fought, and *not* learned overnight. We called upon God's grace and mercy often. And, as often as we asked, His grace and mercy were received.

Over the years, the playhouse was converted into a writing shack for me—an escape place when I needed a breather or a *mom's* time-out from pre-teen's hormones and attitudes. I asked him once why he put the lock on the outside, but Bill's mischievous grin wasn't what I expected. The only answer I received was: "I *might* have done it accidently-on-purpose. Just in case he had to decide if *my* attitude was adjusted enough to be let out!" We laughed over that one. A lot.

The ten acres of property we owned provided adventures and opportunities we never dreamed we'd have. Behind the house on the hill was a small fossil-bed, filled with clams, snails, and other sea treasures and artifacts. Oh, the time spent digging hoping to find buried treasures. When elementary school time arrived, teachers planned field trips to our place so students could dig for fossils and play with our Pygmy goats and chickens, giving them a mini-farm experience. One year the students got to watch as baby pygmy goats were born—a new experience for kids who lived in town, in apartments, or neighborhoods where homes were close together.

Thank goodness for the generous souls in our lives—from our parents, to their friends, to mentors in *Young Life*, and friends in churches who showed us the way to faith with a friendship, a true *relationship* and personal walk with God. I know my reaction of being flipped out over this fixer upper could have tainted our marriage and several friendships as well, if it hadn't been for the love from our friends and God's grace.

I hope you, too, have the value of friends, community, and church family who will surround you—not just in your times of need, but to share in the celebrations and victories won and accomplished!

22

CRASH AND BURN LIGHTLY

On May 10, 1985—right in front of the fixer-upper and my long-dreamt-for log house—I was hit by a drunk driver. It was the Friday before Mother's Day.

A fact I haven't shared yet is we had been praying for, and seriously considering becoming long-term foreign missionaries. So seriously, we had actually applied.

On May the 7th, we found out we had been accepted into the program for foreign missionaries. Then… *wham.*

The accident altered our lives forever.

When it happened, I was at a complete stop, waiting to turn into our driveway. A severely, inebriated driver came barreling behind me. The police later estimated he was going fifty-five miles an hour and never hit his brakes. He was four times the legal limit of alcohol, at 10:30 in the morning.

His car slid down into our hay field, across the road from our house. He suffered no injuries or damages – to himself or to his vehicle.

The impact of the crash was so forceful, my chin and lower jaw hit the steering wheel before my seatbelt had a chance to even engage. Then when it did, my head and neck were jerked back with such force it slammed my head into the back window of my small truck.

In 1985, small trucks were not equipped with headrests or airbags. The result of my face slamming into the steering wheel was quite severe. My jaw joint was jammed, and my cheek bones were shoved up into my eye sockets.

My vision was impacted as blood pooled around the left optic nerve. Double vision and severe migraines still plague me. Three decades plus later, my eye specialist can still see remnants of the optic nerve damage.

But it was so much more than just my face and head. Both shoulders had to be surgically repaired in stages. New technology and surgical techniques became available with each stage. As a result, my rebuilt shoulders are now held up with twenty-five-pound surgical, monofilament fishing line, anchor bolts, screws and titanium.

This was the the beginning of me becoming my own version of the bionic woman.

All in all, I've had more than one hundred surgeries attempting to put Humpty-Dumpty back together again. I wish I could say I have been a perfect patient. You know – a patient full of grace, gratitude, mercy, and especially *patience*. NOT!

There were occasions I wore my emotions on my sleeve. Occasional bursts of anger spewed out of my mouth. My sorrow and grief were accompanied by tears streaming down my cheeks. Our longed-for dreams had been shattered—the first: not being able to bear children due to the DES, and the second: not being able to go on the long-term, foreign mission field. With venom in my tone of voice, I let Bill know how angry I was at God. What kind of God allowed this to happen? Hadn't I been through enough?

I was *more* than angry at the drunk driver. When he hit me it was his *fifth* DUI. He had no liability insurance, and he had multiple liens against his property. This meant we bore the entirety of the financial burden of bills.

I was so full of anger and self-pity I never stopped to think through why the driver felt the need to be drunk at 10:30 in the morning. I couldn't see past my own anger and frustration to remind myself what I knew as an occupational therapist—namely alcohol abuse is often an addiction and illness.

Instead of jail, the driver ended up in a nursing home, due to his alcoholism.

Three short months after the accident, I cringed, feeling a twinge of guilt when I read his obituary in our local paper. He died from cirrhosis of the liver.

Tears pooled in my eyes. Guilt and shame filled me. I dropped to my knees, asking God to forgive me. I also told God I forgave the driver as well.

But my humility was soon replaced with my humanness. I became very self-centered. I wasn't aware or even able to see how the accident affected those around me—especially my family. My physical and occupational therapists often took the brunt of my frustration as I dealt with my loss. The more they encouraged me, even with my rants and rage as I attempted the excruciating exercises they needed to put me through to rehabilitate, the more frustrated I became.

My frustration marched me directly into a season of denial. I made futile attempts trying to perform tasks outside my physical strength and limitations. Over and over again I attempted to groom or lift the saddle onto our daughter's pony. Bill had to be the bad guy and inform me what the therapists had talked to him about—and what I knew as an OT—if I couldn't independently lift and put the saddle on Jamie's pony, named Pal, we couldn't keep him.

I ended up in tears, hurling explicative words into the air. Heads turned when I let loose with four-letter-words and unseemly, salty phrases. I cried a lot, trying to process the physical and emotional pain. I felt like coals were being heaped on me. It also made me feel vulnerable. I didn't want colleagues of mine to be my therapists – even if the gifted therapists were actually my staff members at the rehab center. I had hired each and every one of them. I was their boss when the accident occurred.

Then came insult to injury. The owner of rehab facility reluctantly informed me I needed to step down as Director. I didn't have the physical function or stamina needed to work as a staff therapist much less be the director.

Depression replaced my anger. It crept over me, like a dark cloud. When I realized the magnitude of my losses—physical, financial, career—I hit rock bottom.

I slid deeper into the pit of depression. I didn't care what I looked like and wore the same outfit multiple days in a row. I neglected showering. I slept as often as possible.

Time wore on. Instead of wearing my emotions on my sleeve after receiving unwanted news, I did my best to stuff my feelings of anger, bitterness, hopelessness, and loss inside the deep caverns of my heart until I could stuff no more.

How Bill and Jamie survived is unknown to me. Selfishly, I was in total self-centered focus mode. But thankfully, God was in control. Not me. God gave them patience and endurance beyond measure. His love surrounded Bill and Jamie in ways I never knew until years later.

Then… one day it happened. As the phrase goes, "fertilizer hit the fan." My overflow of toxic waste verbally spewed into the air. It wasn't directed at any one person or situation. It all meshed together. I had completely had it.

I cried. I yelled. I threw pillows against a wall. I even kicked a thin, sheet-rocked wall. I was wearing my heavy-duty hiking boots. The kick was so hard it punched a hole in the wall. Oops!

Bill lovingly looked at me and asked, "Are you done?"

The shock of his question hit me like a ton of bricks. I blinked and stared at him.

With a look of understanding and love, one of his coy, irresistible, and mischievous grins appeared on his face. I knew he had something up his sleeve. His dark chocolate brown eyes twinkled as his vocal pipes broke into song. Improvising the words to the theme music of the classic TV show *Bonanza* he sang:

"Dum-da-da-dumb… *De-ni-al!*"

Finishing his little serenade, he walked toward me, opened his arms to envelope me in warm embrace, and chucked softly. He didn't have to say a word. He *knew* better!

It wasn't the last time I heard him hum or sing his version of the famous theme song over the years. Swallowing pride is not one of my greater gifts. Pushing limits and over-doing are more my style. When life gets tough, when I get tired of being tired, when I am over-the-top, "stick-a-fork-in-me-I'm-done"—living in a state of denial is simply the way I cope on some days.

But life goes on, even when battles rage daily. Thankfully, God is never far away; ready to let us lean into Him fully, with a huge dose of grace and mercy.

Something tells me I'm not alone in this. Can you sing the theme song to *Denial*? I mean…*Bonanza*?

23

MOM AND DAD TO MANY

Humility, much like swallowing my pride, is *not* one of my greater gifts. Life might be easier if it was. Luckily, I had learned a lesson if you don't have a particular gift, and it was needed, a steep learning curve in said area was likely coming down the pike. (It's why I've learned to *not* ask for patience: the answer is sure to be more than I want!)

About a year after we moved into the log house, we had completed a fair amount of the necessary remodeling to make it livable. The labor of love of so many was seen around every corner. We continued to be active in our church, where many of those friends attended as well. We were often asked to help with chaperoning teen events. It was not only fun for us, but Jamie loved the attention the teens drenched her with.

In the years we were involved with the youth group, we became "other mother" or "other dad" to many of the kids. We hadn't bargained for the unexpected lesson on parenting teenagers, but found more often than not, they were seeking affirmation their life mattered. While working with these teens was filled with fun and frolicking, there were some challenging days and some very long nights, when a teen arrived on our doorstep needing to talk. We had gained their trust and we didn't take trust lightly.

Since I was not back to work yet, I was able to help on a "non-school-day" event when parents who worked weren't able to get away. One such event was a day ski-trip. Since Bill had an over-time day of work scheduled on this particular day, I went solo, piling kids and ski equipment into Old Blue.

I stayed in the lodge, finding a comfy spot in front of the fire. When the kids came in, taking a break to warm up or grab a bite to eat, I chit-chatted with them until they hit the slopes again. I was amazed at how openly they shared the battles they were facing and challenges many had going on in their lives. My spot from the fireplace also gave me a good place to keep an eye on the high school kids whose antics when moms and dads weren't around in addition to their raging, roller-coaster hormones could easily get them into trouble.

Overall, the ski trip was amazing. My body was still in rehab mode, and the day pushed it to its utmost limit. By the time I delivered the last teen home, I was exhausted. To say I slept like a log was an understatement.

The next morning, amongst the cobwebs of half-asleep and half-awake, the telephone beside the bed rang. It rang once, twice, then a third time. I *was* going to let it go to the answering machine, but instead, I groaned and decided to pick the phone call up.

The call was from the Office of Children's Services. It was our former case worker, from when we *thought* we might adopt again. That was before our plans to go on the mission field and then the accident occurring. She was talking a million words a minute.

I finally had to interrupt her, "Slow down! I can't catch what you are trying to say."

She stopped talking.

"Could you please start the conversation over and speak a bit slower?" I explained that I wasn't quite awake after a long day chaperoning a teen ski trip.

She took a breath and started over. Apparently our names had come up as the top match in their Child Services system to adopt a five-year-old boy. He was from an abuse and neglect background. He was just now learning to walk and talk. There were some autistic tendencies and mild cerebral palsy—all added to the reasons we came up as a match since I was an occupational therapist and Bill had a coaching and education background from college, as well as a great reputation mentoring boys/teens in the community.

"But I thought we took our name off all adoption lists... almost a year ago. Remember? We were still hoping I might rehab enough for us to go on the mission field.

"What happened?" I didn't understand.

"Well... your name never got removed." She replied in a quiet tone.

There was a long silence on both ends of the phone line.

I finally spoke. "Bill and I *just* told our lawyer we decided we were *not* going to pursue adoption."

She hesitated. I heard her take a deep breath, "Okay... but why don't you come and just see a photo and read his bio, anyway? You might change your mind once you see the picture and read about him."

"No," I told her. I don't dare. Bill was adamant about no more kids He's worried about me as it is... I don't know how we could do it." I apologized again. I wanted and needed to let Bill be the head of the family he had promised to be.

After a few more chit-chat words, we said good-bye.

I slowly rolled out of bed to take a long soak in the hot tub. Sometimes, it was the only way to get my day going.

With eyes closed, I thought about the little boy. I prayed and asked God to find him just the right family.

Next, I did my daily rehab exercises and some general household chores. The entire time, I could not get the phone conversation out of my mind. Finally, five hours after our phone call, I drove the two miles to the Children's Services office and asked to see her. She ushered me into her office, bewildered.

"I thought you said no." She shook her head at me.

"My mouth did, but my heart can't. May I at least see the photo and bio? Then, maybe I can see if Bill is willing?"

I tried *all afternoon* to get the picture and background off my heart, to no avail." I sighed. Looking at the picture, I knew what *my* answer was. Now I had to bring it to Bill…after a lot of prayer and a huge dose of humility to bolster me.

Long story short (you can read more details in *Loose Screws and Skinned Knees*), God blessed us, and we added an incredible son to complete our family.

The way every little piece fell together was as equally miraculous as the adoption events that occurred seven years earlier with our daughter's adoption. This time though, the adoption was through a state-run agency. It ended up involving people from seven different states, including multiple people whose paths had crisscrossed with ours over the years in ways not even *remotely* related to adoption.

We believe our two adoptions could only have happened by the grace, providence, and hand of God. As the years pass, new details pop up about both adoptions from people. Sometimes in places we could never imagine. As each new piece of information is received, we learn another lesson in humility. The occurrences could not have been—in any way, shape, or form—put together by mere man. They came from no other source than the One who has known us before we were in our mothers' wombs, the very God who has counted every hair on our heads, and numbered each of our days.

We knew God had heard the cries of our hearts. He had seen every tear shed in secret and bottled them. He had a plan. It was a plan inconceivable by the world's standards.

Our adoptions are reminders God is in *all* the details, *all* the time. That's just who God is. He has been by our side as we raised our two wonderful kids. We were grateful for our unexpected prep time and experience with the teens He gave us the opportunity to work with—every moment was needed.

We found as we raised our own kids, we discovered each child comes with their own bents, attitudes, gifts, and abilities. Our kids also had special needs requiring extra help, *and* they had a mom who was in a perpetual state of battling medical issues or surgeries. We needed those "other" moms and dads in our *own* lives.

Kids often listen to someone *other* than their own parent—even if we said the exact same thing in the exact same way.

Our kids' terrible twos stage turned into trying teens, which then turned into the most challenging season we faced. We called it: "The taxing times of the twenty-somethings."

Funny, how many people I talk to agree, once our kids make it past the teens and enter make it into their third decade, they begin to think parents magically have a half ounce of sense. And, maybe, just might admit parents are right on occasion! (But don't expect them to fess up to it. They'll deny every word!)

Reaching out to the younger generation, listening, laughing, praying, and sharing with them by walking your talk, by showing them they are valued and cared for will allow them to be ready for the everyday battles they face. Technology, gaming, vaping, drugs, being bullied are all battles they face. These battlefields seem much greater than previous generations have faced – or at the very least different. Our job is to help them to stand ready to stay the course. Their armor may have some chinks in it, but hey, they can help us find the TV remote and show us how to use our phones and computers!

24

GENERATIONAL LOVE

Four months after our son's adoption was final, our family was to be blessed with even more family.

My (deceased) grandmother's younger sister—my maternal-great-aunt—was living in Southern California at the time of Tim's adoption. Her beloved husband, Johnny, had died a year prior, after a horrific battle with pancreatic cancer. We worried about her living alone. She lived literally two blocks from several large movie studios. She had to contend with their tourist attraction crowds, high traffic volume and mayhem. Worried about her welfare, we called her weekly.

Aunt Betty never learned to drive. She was in the habit of walking to the corner market if she needed anything. She refused any of our efforts to help her. On multiple occasions we had extended an offer to come live with us knowing she'd thrive. But Aunt Betty was a proud woman *and* extremely independent.

After one of our weekly phone calls, I hung up the phone and floated an idea to Bill. What if we used the ploy of asking Aunt Betty to move and live with us to help *us*? It wasn't a coy tactic—I really could use her help. I was still in the midst of my rehab from being hit by the drunk driver. I could use an extra adult hand around the house during the day.

On our next weekly phone call, we shared our idea with her. To our surprise, she agreed with an exuberant "Yes!" We were taken off guard, but were delighted.

Within weeks, Bill made the drive to Southern California and packed her up. It was decided it would be easier for her to fly up, instead of the long drive. After making sure she was safely on her flight, Bill made a non-stop drive home, pulling a small trailer with her few belongings. He arrived home only twelve short hours after she did.

Our lives were enriched having three generations living under one roof. Dinner time often ended with Aunt-Betty-time when she entertained us with stories of growing up in the early 1900's. We had to… *ahem*… edit a couple of her stories of being a flapper girl in the 1920's and other escapades that era provided, but we never tired of her stories, which were delightful and history lessons for all of us. She brought much laughter as she scooted her roly-poly frame, hollering, "Eww! Eww!" when she saw a spider crawling up a wall or as she attempted to get out of the infamous Pacific Northwest rain.

Just as she introduced us to decades and activities we had not known, we reciprocated with activities *she* had never participated in. Believe it or not (with the help of Bill's scuba weight belt attached), we got her roly-poly, bobbing body into our hot tub a time or two. Imagine the squeals of delight as she rode on a snowmobile on her 90th birthday!

Aunt Betty was not to escape the genetic scourge of cancer that hit and continues to plague many of our family members. While living with us, Aunt Betty was diagnosed with malignant bilateral breast cancer, requiring a double mastectomy. We moved a hospital bed into the living room and placed her favorite floral quilt over it. She could rest while the kids were at school. I was able to help with her therapy exercises as I did my therapy regime as well. While it wasn't her first choice of where to have her bedroom, it did allow her to be in the center of all the activities going on—and let me tell you, she never missed a beat.

After her victorious battle with breast cancer, Aunt Betty grew stronger and became more empowered than ever. One evening after the kids were in bed, she asked to talk to Bill and me. She told us she wanted to live on her own again. After all, the kids were heading into their pre-teens and she knew they could be more than a handful. Adding their social and athletic events made for a very busy schedule for her to keep up with. "I'm no spring chicken anymore," she often stated.

She wanted to look into living in a senior apartment complex about two miles from our house. The apartment was only blocks from where the kids went to school. It was close enough for frequent after school visits to munch on Oreos™ together and yet far enough away she could feel independent. Independence was an important desire of hers.

We agreed to support her in her goal of living alone again, assuring her she was always welcome to move back, if she changed her mind, or any situations changed.

She was elated when an apartment became available.

Aunt Betty knew several senior women from attending our church and the Senior Sunday School and socials, who were already living in the same independent–living apartment complex. It was a special time for our family to get to know them, hearing even *more* turn of the century tales. Aunt Betty was the youngest of the group, so the stories went back to the late 1800's!

"The Girls" is how Aunt Betty referred to her group of the four, eighty-to-ninety year-old plus seniors. On a weekly basis, they made their way to their favorite restaurant. Hunched and hobbled, they somehow all got into Gladys's (the eldest of the group) red Chevy sedan. Canes and walkers included. Age had taken its physical toll on each of them. Their heads could barely be seen over the driver's steering wheel or seat-backs.

As the infamous red Chevy crawled at a snail's pace down the main drag of town, *everyone* knew to give them *plenty* of space on the road. We dared not ask how in the world Gladys got her license renewed each year!

Those whose lives intersected with these ladies were blessed by their gift of generational love and care. Their sage, timely advice, their godly words of wisdom and discernment, their bold living out and sharing their life experiences, and their deep, deep faith in God, continues to abide in us—long after they left this world to be in their heavenly Home.

Seeds were planted in our lives as they shared their stories and testimonies. They fell on hungry young hearts—fertile soil. The fruits of the seeds they planted in our lives are a reminder to be faithful, just like "The Girls." It is now our turn to share, mentor, and plant seeds in hungry young lives God brings across *our* paths. As we pass on the lessons of generational love we learned, sharing stories of courage, faith, hard work, and daily battles victoriously fought, we are also teaching them how to not wimp out.

Who are you passing lessons of life to?

25

BATTLE READY

I wish I could tell every reader and every person I've spoken to, life will be easy.

But I can't. Because it isn't.

We *all* face our own normal. For us, some of the normal experiences over the years were abject warfare and full on battles.

We have had to overcome financial obstacles. We have faced unanticipated medical battles that certainly weren't outlined in our wedding vows. And, our kids have daily battled their own special needs and faced their own warfare.

Thankfully, the churches we've been a part of have taught sound principles and doctrine about spiritual warfare. It helped us learn early in our marriage how to deal with warfare when it hit. Notice I wrote *when*. Not *if*. Because I promise… it *will* hit.

"The enemy only picks a fight or battle with someone who is a threat to his agenda." Do you believe that statement to be true? Bill and I do. It's something we have clung to over the years. We know we're a threat. In fact, it's been a goal of ours.

Each time we encountered spiritual warfare we called it out for what it was. No matter what ploy Satan tried, as long as we stood firm on and in God's Word, we knew he was destined to lose. No matter how hard the battle was, no matter what ground or area the battles take place, (spiritual, emotional, physical, financial, or a combination) we *knew* Satan will lose.

Satan *is* a loser!

We have fought long and hard. Stories in *Loose Screws* and the words you are reading in *Don't Wimp Out* chronicle some of the battles we have fought…and *won*.

We have the advantage of garrisons and legions of angels forming a hedge of protection around us—because our names are written in the Lamb's Book of Life, and the Blood of Jesus, spilled out on Good Friday sealed our victory. Bill and I are grateful we grew up with people who loved and cared enough for us to teach us about spiritual warfare–Sunday School teachers, youth group leaders, family, and later in life friends and other mentors who crossed our path.

When the kids were elementary school age, one particular Sunday school lesson taught them about spiritual warfare and the importance of the daily need to put on the armor of God, spoken about in the Bible. (Ephesians 6:13-18).

The kids thoroughly enjoyed the participatory activity of "putting on the armor of God" their teacher taught them. The kids were adamant we needed to do the activity daily.

So, before the kids left for school, I'd go through the morning check-list: Back pack? Check. Gym clothes? Check. Library books? Check. Lunch? Check. Teeth brushed? With their eyes rolling in unison they groaned, "Check, Mom."

"So the last but most important thing we have to do is what?" I asked.

"Put our armor on!!" The kids exclaimed, jumping up and down. (I'm sure it was much more fun than the checklist I had just gone over!)

We went through the motions of putting on their armor. We started with them placing their hand on top of their heads for the helmet of salvation—they knew God was with them. Then they picked up their imaginary (but very real in their actions!) Sword of the Spirit—a reminder of God's special, and personal Word to them. They acted out putting on a breast-plate of righteousness to help them make good and right choices. They cinched on a belt of Truth, reminding them to *always* be honest. Next, they put on the shoes of readiness so they were at peace, and knowing they were ready for *any*thing they encountered during the day. Last, but far from least, they picked up their Shield of Faith, knowing they were prepared to fight off any arrows the enemy tried to shoot at them. They knew and believed they could always pray—whether it was out loud or in their hearts—and God heard every word and stood ready to come to their aid.

To this day, our kids can recite putting on the armor. On numerous occasions they shared their gratefulness for being prepared and dressed in their armor. We were also grateful because there were some battles we couldn't prepare them for or even explain.

26

YOU'VE BEEN SERVED

We were still in the season where Bill was the primary bread-winner and I worked my way back from the car accident through rehab. One afternoon, after arriving home from picking the kids up from school, I heard a knock at the front door.

Opening it, I saw a man I'd never seen before.

"Mrs. Tuk?" His face held no expression.

"Yes, may I help you?"

He extended his arm and handed me an envelope. "You've been served." And he turned around, walked down the still-crumbling porch steps, and drove away, all before I could utter a word.

Served? What did *that* mean? Surely it couldn't mean like a scene out of *Perry Mason*. The envelope looked rather official and daunting. I decided to wait until Bill got home from work to open it. Boy… was *that* the right decision.

After dinner and getting the kids off to bed, Bill and I opened the envelope.

We were being sued!

We stared at each other in shock. My stomach was suddenly in my throat. I could tell by the red creeping up Bill's neck and face, he was about to explode in anger.

Sued? For what?

As we read through the document and did our best to decipher legal-ese, we realized what the lawsuit was about, and why we were being sued.

In the aftermath of the Mount St. Helens eruption, Bill and an acquaintance accepted a small job to fix a building that had been damaged by the flooding after Mount St. Helens eruption and the volcanic ash.

The job required a thirty day bond as insurance. Bill and I had agreed to do our best to never borrow money, except for a mortgage or car loan. We waffled back and forth at the time about entering into a bond situation. In the end, we rationalized we could really use the money from this particular side-job, especially with my mounting medical bills, and our expected moving expenses.

Bill knew his friend needed the job for his family just as badly as we did—if not worse. He had completely lost his business when the volcano blew. We thought this job was an answer to prayer for both families. Since the bond was only for thirty days, we felt in this *one* instance it was okay to take out the bond. Besides, as soon as this job was complete, we were moving north.

The men completed the job in *less* than thirty days. They were handsomely paid for the job done, plus they each received a bonus for finishing the job early. It was an unexpected financial blessing.

Fast forward two years. We were settling into the log house.

Never in a million years could we have imagined Bill's acquaintance would use the short-term bond without notifying us. Several days before the thirty day bond was due to expire, he had not only used the bond to take on a large project, but he walked off the job, leaving us holding the financial and legal bag.

The amount we were being sued for was more than twice what we had ever made in a year. We felt sucker-punched. We tried every way we knew to get in touch with the co-signer. But it was like he had vanished into thin air. Even his family didn't know how to reach him.

We sought legal advice. After discussion with our lawyer, we forlornly realized we *were* liable. Legal bills were to be added to our budget for quite some time. The bright side of this malady was our lawyer explained to the people behind the lawsuit about what had *truly* transpired. They, in turn, proposed a settlement offer to us. While it was a gracious offer—and one we took—it still put a strain on our financial portfolio, limited as it was.

I was mad. No, I was more than mad. I was angry. Bill felt like a failure, and I didn't want him to feel worse than he already did. I knew the only place to go was to take my anger about the whole situation to God in prayer.

I told God I didn't think it was fair. It was hard being accused and held accountable for something we didn't do. Much less even knew about. Were we *so* naïve or so gullible? After all, we had no reason *not* to trust Bill's acquaintance. Yes, we *did* sign the bond, which was legally binding for thirty days, regardless of any party defaulting. I whined to God, trying to reason with Him and explain how it should be – at least according to me. Ever patient, God let me vent, whine, cry, and be angry. I sat on the side of my bed in silence. My gaze landed on the nightstand where my Bible lay.

Sigh…I knew His answer to my cries were to be found in His Word.

I randomly opened my well-worn and underlined Bible. My eyes landed on Matthew 5:44: "Love your enemies and pray for those who persecute you." (NLV)

They weren't exactly the words I wanted to read at the moment.

I sat on the bed seriously considering what the verse meant in light of the situation. I couldn't fathom we were left in this predicament, unless something dire had happened. If their family didn't know how to get in contact with them, the situation must be serious. I thought about their three teenagers. I wondered how they were coping with whatever was going on. Surprisingly, I found myself praying for each person in their family. I prayed for protection, for wisdom, for peace.

This was warfare. I could feel it. We just had to keep believing and wearing the armor we daily put on.

After I finished praying, I felt a nudge—the kind I have come to know was from The One who cares. Even though our lawyer had found the address where the person who left us holding the bill was now living, he advised us we were to have no face-toface or voice contact with them.

I couldn't ignore the nudge. Our lawyer didn't say anything about a card. I felt compelled to drop a note of encouragement to the family, right after I wrote the monthly check to pay for our legal agreement responsibility. I strongly felt *not* to mention the situation, nor to use any Christian platitudes or Scripture. Just drop two or three lines in a card, letting them know we were thinking of them, and hoping things were okay.

I was faithful to the nudge each month, writing a letter to the family, right after I wrote the check to the legal firm—for the *five years* it took us to pay off our legal responsibility. At first it was painstakingly hard. But as the months and years went on, my heart softened and I actually looked forward to dropping a note of encouragement – even though we *never* heard back from them.

That is, not until four years *after* our financial obligation was met.

I went to the mailbox as I usually did mid-afternoon. In the mail, was a hand-written letter with a return address of a military academy. I was puzzled, since we didn't know of anyone who was affiliated with the military academy at the time. I opened the letter. As I read the first line, I knew I better sit down.

The letter had come from the eldest son of Bill's acquaintance—the one who had walked away from the job, the bond, and future financial obligations. Tears filled my eyes and spilled down my cheeks as I read the contents of the letter. The son was thanking us for showing him and his sibling what true Christians looked like.

He went on to explain he read *every* letter I had written, every note of encouragement. He had been baffled. He knew his parents had egregiously wronged us, even hurt us, yet we were able to look beyond and offer words of comfort at a time when they were all hurting and confused. He explained his dad had sunk into a deep depression after Mount St. Helens blew. His dad had literally lost his entire life's savings and work. They were living in a small travel trailer behind their truck. We had never been privy to the details—we only knew they had been hit hard when the mountain blew.

He went on to say in his dad's depression, haunting memories of serving in the Vietnam War re-surfaced for his dad, making matters even worse. His mom did her best to protect the kids, but the severe depression, violent outbursts, and little food were hard to keep hidden. He wrote our notes were his family's life-line, a buoy if you will, when they all felt like they were drowning for sure.

He quizzically related how we knew the *exact* words to say. He share how the notes always came on the *exact* needed day and were the exact words of encouragement needed to give them hope to keep going for another day.

The son wrote, "You know my family is Catholic. We believe in God. But you, Bill and Care, showed us who God *really* is—a person who loves and cares for you no matter what. You showed us what God's forgiveness looks like in real life. You never once mentioned God's name, you never added a Scripture verse, and you just loved on our family. I am forever changed because of you, and I wanted you to know. You showed me the difference of a "going to church type Christian" and a person who "walks out their faith and doesn't just believe *in* God, but *believes* God. And not being some Bible-banger, or going to Mass and confession every week.

"I hope you get this letter. I needed to tell you your notes and prayers kept our family together during our darkest times. We are so grateful for your love, your understanding, your prayers, and living out who God really is. I pray for you often, and apologize for what happened. I know it wasn't right. I know it wasn't fair. I know it probably made things really, really hard for you. Thank you for being willing to forgive my mom and dad. I know us kids do—because we know God wants us to. You taught us about goodness and mercy. We will remember and carry it with us for the rest of our lives."

He closed the letter with a military-type, proper, and precise conclusion signature.

Warfare… it comes in all shapes, sizes, situations, and places. Like a nation's military, those of us who are in "God's Army" must always be prepared. We never know when a battle may break out. The Good News is, we *know* Who wins the battle when all is said and done.

27

WATER, WATER EVERYWHERE – LOWER 48 STYLE

I've got a question for you. If you lived in an area in the one-hundred-year flood plain, and there were five floods, you'd be 500-years old, right?

Hypothetically speaking of course.

But truth being told, we often wondered.

We joked when the heavens opened up and let loose with rain maybe Bill *should* start building an ark. After all, if we go by flood-years (you know, like dog-years), we were in the age range of Noah. Noah was 600-years old when the floodwaters arrived, and it was around 120 years from the time Noah heard God's assignment of the ark until the arrival of the rain. Talk about patience and obedience.

Luckily, we only had front row seats to the floods in SW Washington. During our time in the log home, there were floods in November 1986, January 1990, February 1990, November 1990, and April 1991. In each of the five high-water situations and/or floods, our acreage and hay field flooded, but the water was held at bay by a high bank leading from the hay field, up to the road, and our house across the street. Each time the freeway was under water, trooper's rerouted traffic up and over several meandering backroads including the road in front of our house.

We never realized how many tractor-trailer and eighteen-wheeler trucks travelled the freeway during the middle of the night! Frequently we woke up from the noise from truckers using their noisy, window-rattling Jake-brake as they down-shifted their heavy load. More than likely forgetting they weren't on a freeway anymore. It must have been quite the ordeal attempting to slow down to the twenty-five mph speed limit as they approached the city limits. We surmised more times than not, the infractions by the truckers were unintentional. We figured instead of grousing about it, we'd cut the truckers some slack, knowing it was a short-term nuisance and rectified once the freeway opened back up. After all, we remembered the days Bill and his dad drove big rigs, and how easy it was to forget to *not* use the Jake-brake as they approached city limits.

While our home and property had no flood-water damage, we were still very much affected by the floods. When the high waters hit flood stage, the areas and towns around the area were closed down. In 1986 and 1990, the kids' schools flooded, our church flooded, several grocery stores and businesses flooded. It was a mess.

Several of our friends' homes had significant water damage. Thankfully, Aunt Betty and "The Girls'" apartment complex were spared. Water only came up to their porches and not inside their ground level living space.

Bill spent many hours helping at the church sump-pumping water out of the lower floor. He would 'tag-team' with other folks as they tried to save office supplies, school books/ curriculum in the Christian School and Sunday school rooms, or tearing down wet sheet rock. The group of men who banded together to help were featured on local news. It didn't faze them as news helicopters flew overhead, circling the church and flooded area collecting footage for the evening news. Hours turned into days for Bill and the others who slogged through the flood damage and water. The men were divided into groups, each shift working six to eight hours, working around each person's regular job.

Because of Bill's construction skills and not being able to get to jobs sites until the waters receded, he often offered to pull double shifts as they worked to repair the damage. He would come home exhausted. Chilled to the bone, he headed straight for a *hot* shower, put on *dry* clothes, grabbed a quick bite to eat, and before I knew it, he was out like a light, snoring loudly nestled in the comfort of our heated waterbed and warm comforter. This routine lasted for two weeks straight.

As he left home for one of his final flood shifts, Bill looked across the valley where we lived. He saw an arching *double* rainbow.

Bill looked heavenward and said, "I hope this rainbow means a promise for no more rain anytime soon, otherwise I *will* start building an ark!"

28

SPLISH-SPLASH

Bill continued to keep busy with the aftermath of the floods. His carpentry skills were in high demand. While Bill pounded away with a hammer, I pounded the pavement with my feet. I was on the hunt for find new ways to incorporate my "for-the-rest-of-my-life" therapy routines and exercises into functional activities. I wanted to place the emphasis on the *fun* in functional. If I couldn't have fun as I performed the monotonous exercises, I might have given up exercising all together.

One activity I started building into my schedule was going to the indoor community pool at the early morning hour of 5:30 a.m. I swam laps and did my personal adaptive swim exercises, much like I had taught others when I was Director of Swim Rehab at the YMCA™, years earlier.

I was taking a breather between kickboard laps one morning when the pool manager approached me. He knew me not only as a regular at early morning lap time, but I was an occasional substitute swim teacher when they needed someone in a pinch. The manager and I engaged in small talk, and then he changed to a more serious tone of voice. Apparently, some parents had been talking to him, along with local area school districts' athletic directors, proposing an idea about starting up an age-group swim team.

Aware of my resume and aquatic background, he asked me

what I thought of the idea. I enthusiastically replied it was a *wonderful* idea and needed addition to the community. It could offer kids not involved in main-stream sports like football, basketball, baseball, or dance an opportunity to be involved in a sport whose parameters were individually tailored to their skill set. It meant you could have kids as young as six-years-old up through high school age. Kids with disabilities could participate as well. I saw it as a win-win possibility.

When I was chatting with the manager at the o-dark-thirty time of day, my brain was not fully engaged. I was in lap-counting mode besides getting my therapy exercises completed so I could rush home in time to get the kids up and off to school. What I failed to comprehend at the moment was the manager of the pool was quizzing me with an ulterior motive.

About five minutes after I had left the pool, my brain now fully awake and engaged, I realized what the pool manager was *actually* asking. The guy had clearly been digging to see if I'd be willing to develop and implement the swim team!

Bill greeted me when I drove in the driveway. I asked him if he had a minute before he left for work to share my morning's conversation with the pool manager. Luckily, he did.

We sat down on the *still* crooked cement porch steps of the log house. We both agreed it was a no-brainer type of decision. While I wasn't physically ready to return to a full-time job in the occupational therapy field, I *could* weave my OT skills, my swim background, plus do my physical therapy exercises as I coached. The timing couldn't have been more perfect.

Bill joked he'd had enough water experience with the flood(s) *he* might be qualified for the job. But then quickly added he was *more* than happy to hand any duties that involving water back to me. It was a position, if offered, I'd love to take. If I was offered the job, we'd be given a free family membership to the pool. An added bonus would be our daughter, who displayed natural swimming talent especially in the breast stroke, could be part of the swim-team at no cost to us.

As Bill and I said our good-byes for the day, the phone rang. It was the pool manager.

"Hey Care, just calling to ask if you understood what I was *really* talking to you about this morning." Not giving me a chance to reply, he continued, "Since you are doing so much better and looking for something to do, how about starting up a swim team for the community?"

I chuckled, telling the manager, "By the time I got home, I put two and two together and I have already talked to Bill about it. If the community is willing to take a chance on me, I am willing to do my best to pull an area swim team together."

So began Lewis County Aquatics Swim Team. Utilizing my skills as an occupational therapist, my credentials in aquatics, and the expertise I had gained developing and implementing new therapy programs, I started the program from scratch. We started small, with about ten to fifteen regulars. Once word got out, the numbers grew at a rapid pace. At one time, the team had over seventy members, ranging in age from six to eighteen years old.

I would coach five days a week, for two to three hours. My heart was full as I watched kids from varied backgrounds and abilities splish-splash away. I liked to keep the monotony of solely doing timed laps and regimented skill drills to make the cut-off time needed to enter a competition.

I livened up workouts with games like *Wheels of Workout*— where the team captain of each age section spun a wheel revealing a particular work-out set. Swimmers groaned as inevitably the workouts they spun for were *much* more intense or difficult than many of my planned workouts! We played *Marco Polo*, or bring out water balls for *Deep End Dodge Ball*, which was played in the cordoned off deep end, where they had to tread water the entire game.

Often the team didn't realize I had a method to my madness when I prepared the varied work-out schedule. They didn't realize I was actually having them cross-training, working on building up specific muscle groups.

For several of the work-outs, I had swimmers tie rubber tubing around above their knees, or use Theraband™ to do arm stretches, or do three-ten minute intervals knee high running in the kiddie pool. Even game day had a specific purpose. They eventually pleaded with me *not* to play *Walk Down – Swim Back*, a game where they would dive off the starting blocks in the shallow end, swim their choice of stroke for twenty-five meters, pulling themselves up on the deck (no stairs or pool ladders allowed!) for the entire workout hour. It was meant to develop not only their favorite stroke, but taught them how to pace. Boy did they have and complain about sore muscles the next day!

Since I was coaching multiple age groups a with multiple skill levels, it was important to me to encourage each swimmer to do *their* best—not someone else's best. I knew the better swimmers with faster times could help the younger, less talented swimmers. I especially wanted the team to know, without a shadow of a doubt, the word t-e-a-m had no letter I in it. It meant we were all in this together. I fostered an environment of encouraging each other, showing respect, building each other up, and reminding each individual of their special and unique abilities. It was important to me to teach and affirm each one of my swimmers: when things got tough, or they were tired and wanted to quit, not to wimp out. To reinforce that affirmation I would monthly drop each swimmer a personal, hand-written note, letting them know how proud I was of them and the hard work they were putting in.

The "Guppies" (younger swimmers) looked forward to the

work-out days they were paired up with a "Dolphin" (older swimmers). The workout was split in half, where each swimmer got to a take turn coaching the other. What a hoot to watch the younger ones coach!

Being a *functional* coach, I was often found in the water during work-outs. It was easier on my body for one, and secondly, being in the water I could submerse myself and analyze a swimmer's stroke, their kicking style or area needing bit of tweaking.

I had a philosophy I'd never ask a swimmer to do something I, too, was not willing to do, within their range of capabilities. The only exception I made to that philosophy was the workouts for three High School Exchange Students I had the second year I coached. One swimmer was from Spain, one from Japan, and the swimmer from Sweden was preparing for the Olympic Time Trials. Needless to say, *their* workouts were *well* above my pay grade! I was grateful for their coach's foresight to send work-out schedules with them. Interpreting them was a different story—language gaps are a real thing.

Many weekends were spent travelling to regional swim meets, as our local pool had not been credentialed yet for the numbers of people who attended or participated in a regular swim meet. There were usually six to ten different teams at any one meet. It made for great camaraderie when families caravanned to other pools, often pitching tents so swimmers could rest or stay out of the sun in between their events and for times when we literally camped out for a two-day event. I still hear from some of my swimmers and the story often comes up how they never forgot the 2:00 a.m. wake-up call when the host club forgot to turn the automatic sprinklers off and their tents went air-borne.

Once again, I was blessed by being *paid* to do something I *loved*. And, I was gaining more of my physical stamina back. Even though I wasn't working technically as an OT, I was using

the knowledge and many techniques I'd gained as an occupational therapist. God answered the desire of my heart in a way I could
never imagine. My cup was filled to over-flowing. I was filled with
joy unspeakable.

I'd say splish-splash fit the category of putting the *fun* back in
function—don't you?

What fun do *you* put in your functional everyday life? If you
haven't tried it yet, there's no better time to start than right now!

29

SUPER TROOPERS

Just as the flood waters ebbed, so did my days of twice weekly sessions of physical and occupational therapy. Once I started coaching the local swim team, being in the water became my therapy.

Therapy or not, I was not to escape my nemesis of my exposure to DES. During the years spanning from 1984-1994, I dealt with two separate battles with cancer—one in the form of breast cancer, the other in thyroid cancer. To make things more interesting, I suffered degenerative joint disease, especially in my knees. The cancers were caught in their early stages, so thankfully I did not have to do chemo or radiation. After multiple surgeries to attempt to repair the meniscus in my right knee, repair damaged tendons and ligaments, plus surgeries to clean up scar tissue, the joint disease in my right knee finally necessitated a total knee replacement.

At forty years of age, I was considered far too young for optimal long-term surgical outcomes, but the orthopedists had little choice. My right knee was disintegrating rapidly. Physicians have told me multiple times over the years despite the incredulous number of medical mazes we have walked through, my medical knowledge as an OT, plus knowing and paying attention to my body, I totally defy the logic of modern medicine. What? Thirty-six surgeries on one leg and over 120 total surgeries (so far) are defying the odds?!

I told the doctors and surgeons it helped having the Great Physician as my medical team leader. After all, it was He who knew me and my parts before I was ever born! (Note: No, I'm not saying God *caused* any of my medical/surgical issues. After all, it was my parents' decision to try the drug DES to give me a chance at the wonderful life I've lived. The side effects causing most of my medical problems were unknown at the time of their decision.)

I believe God has chosen to work *through* each of my DES related situations. In the school of hard knocks, I was learning lessons of pacing, humility, asking for help when needed, patience (mostly with myself), and yes, even joy. I learned first-hand how God uses lessons *I* needed to help others as *they* journeyed through medical mazes and situations of their own.

With all my surgeries and rehab, our kids had to help pick up the slack. They were super troopers. They stepped up, assuming responsibilities at a much younger age than those of their peers. I mean, what seven-year-old boy *willingly* sorts family laundry into whites, colors, heavily stained (and smelly!), work and sports uniforms? What nine-year-old girl will put the sorted clothes into the washer at the correct settings, with the correct amount of detergent, and then put them into the dryer for the needed time? Whose kids actually folded *and* put the loads of laundry they did together *away*? Yep. You got it. Mine!

To show the kids our appreciation, we wanted to shower them with an age appropriate surprise.

The first piece of Bill's and my secret plan was to schedule my total knee surgery for *after* their Spring Break. Next, we arranged to take them out of school three days before the break was to begin. The teachers agreed instead of taking regular class assignments with them, they could create their own book, regaling tales of the journey they took. Once school was back in session, the teachers set time aside for the kids' to share their book with their peers, complete with photos, geographic and scientific facts gleaned and fun had.

On the night we were to leave, it seemed to take the kids *forever* to fall completely asleep. Once we were positively sure they were asleep, I brought out the packed suitcases from their hiding place while Bill loaded sleeping bags and pillows, clipboards to write on, word game books, maps to follow along with, and of course, a cooler filled with copious amounts of snacks and drinks for the journey.

Once the car was ready, we abruptly woke the kids up. When they groggily asked where we were going, we told them an urgent trip had come up, and they needed to come with us. Thankfully, they were still drowsy enough to not ask further questions, and blearily climbed into the back seat of our car.

Once on the road, the kids quickly fell back asleep. Bill and I took turns throughout the next eighteen hours and drove straight from to our place to Anaheim, California. Our daughter woke up about the time we crossed the California border. It didn't take her long to figure out where we were headed. She jostled her brother awake, unable to contain her excitement.

While she guessed where we were headed, her younger brother needed several hints. The first hint we gave was: "One of the people is really, really small. Like mini-small." Another hint was: "Another person we have to see is a really, really, goofy."

Our son, flabbergasted, yelled out, "We're going to Disneyland™! I've waited my *whole life* for this!" (He was all of seven at the time.)

A good time was had by all. Three days at the famous theme park filled our hearts and blistered our feet. The drive home was not an eighteen-hour-marathon-drive like on the way down, but a nice meander up Highway 101—the Pacific Coast Highway. We stopped to view the humungous, historic redwood trees, wandered through sea lion caves and played in the tide-pools of Haystack Rock at Cannon Beach, Oregon. The kids diligently worked on their daily journal, excited to get back to school to share it with their classmates.

All too soon the *real* fun ended. The kids settled back in school. They shared their books with their classmates and enjoyed being the center of attention to their envious peers.

A short week home from our extravaganza, Bill and I shared with our "super troopers" we were headed for another round of our "normal" routine. I explained the knee surgery and rehab afterwards. Luckily, therapy for a total knee was *much* shorter than injuries sustained in the car accident. Family, friends, and co-workers pitched in, helping with meals and carpools as needed. The kids knew they never had to walk this path alone: family, friends, and a God who loved them dearly, had their backs.

It is not always easy to step up to the plate, especially when you aren't given a choice. Sometimes all you can do is face hard situations head-on—even when you are just a kid.

Super Troopers… ya gotta love 'em!

30

TOOLBOX TIPS

High waters and splashing aside, the days, months, and years as the kids became pre-teens were more than eventful. The compilation of events we walked through stretched our faith, tried our patience with each other, and taxed the overall family daily schedule. Something had to give. There was so much to do and so little time!

We decided to use a color-coded calendar to keep dates, times, and activities straight and *hopefully* make the days a bit less stressful. I grabbed a variety of colored pens from the pen and pencil jar. I asked the kids, Bill, and Aunt Betty to each choose a pen to be their color on the calendar and then I took one for myself.

Each person's activity or appointment was to be written only in their color on the over-size calendar hanging on the corkboard wall in what I lovingly referred to as, "Kitchen Central." It didn't take long for the plain white calendar to turn into a bright, rainbow-colored piece of family artwork. It was a delicate, yet challenging juggling act to make sure the right person got to the right event at the right time, on the right day. The brightly-colored calendar helped turn busy, jumbled days into organized chaos. Especially the days where we needed to be in two or three places at the same time. The kids called these days "double-do" or "triple-play" days. Days which happened more often than *any* of us preferred.

While the color-coding technique reduced some of the stress, I could tell when family priorities were getting muddled and pre-set boundaries were being stretched taut to their absolute limits. Tempers could often become testy, words became daggers, and decibel levels rose exponentially when schedules and priorities got out of kilter.

Bill and I recognized we needed to pull more from our parenting and family toolbox. The box held techniques, ideas, and strategies shared by friends, family, colleagues, parents, and elders who had travelled the parenthood path ahead of us. Their tips were invaluable. They shared ideas that worked and others that hadn't worked for them as well.. The failed tools were still kept in the toolbox, as our friends and mentors said they found what doesn't work for one family member or situation just might be the best answer for another. Their words of wisdom came with the admonishment and reminder each child was different, just as every situation is different. Each had their own personality, gifts, and needs.

Truer words have never been spoken.

When we commiserated, "Kids don't come with a manual," our friends and mentors all told us we were gravely mistaken. There was a time-honored parenting and self-help life manual. It has been (and still is) on multiple best-sellers lists. The book you ask?

The Bible.

Friends shared the tool of *The Good Book* (The Bible) held answers and so much more. We just needed to spend time reading it. They recommended we should read it daily. They also recommended re-reading it, studying it, underline and memorize verses, and cling to the promises and answers that jumped out at us.

Our friends shared there was also a "24/7 Help Line," where you are *never* put on hold. The name of that tool was called Prayer. All *we* had to do was talk and share with the person on the other line—God—the Ultimate Parent. He was on-call, ever-present, and available. We would never get a busy signal or a voice mail message. All we had to do was ask. The line was always open 24/7.

What are some of your favorite tools in your family's toolbox?

31

ALL FOR ONE AND ONE FOR ALL

As we continued to rummage through our toolbox, we came upon a tool we knew other families had successfully used. Several families found as their lives continued to get busier and attitudes reflected tired and testy times, a "Family Time Out" was in order. The technique/tool was called "Family Night."

Those who had gone before us, made sure we understood Family Night required a firm, unyielding commitment and continuity to be successful. Each family member had to be present to make it work.

Our friends were right. It *did* take time, commitment, and continuity to implement. It seemed awkward at first. We chose to keep Family Night to just the four of us, a decision Aunt Betty agreed with. She agreed to be our referee if needed, and we included her on nights where special activities were chosen.

The basic premise of Family Night was one night per week, after homework was finished until around dinner time until bedtime, we spent time together. We took the telephone off the hook, pagers were silenced, and all other commitments cancelled or rescheduled. The *only* time a Family Night was rescheduled was for illness or if an activity beyond our control came up…like a school concert, where mandatory attendance was required. For us, we chose a consistent night that typically had the least activity. Typically it was Tuesday night.

The next premise we implemented was fun. Each individual was responsible and in charge of one Family Night a month. With a family of four it worked out perfectly. The person in charge would choose the dinner menu, and decided what family activity we partook in. Part of the planning necessitated pre-planning a week in advance. Each person made a list of items and ingredients needed for their special night. They created a budget, planned and arranged a time to go grocery shopping for menu items they needed. No surprise, many of the nights when the kids were in charge, the menu leaned toward tacos, pizza, or macaroni and cheese! The person in charge was responsible for not just planning, but making the meal itself. All four food groups were to be included, and we all agreed it *must* include a dessert!

This was a great opportunity to reinforce reading and math skills, basic budgeting, and the nuances of grocery shopping. It served to highlight the need for a plan, sticking to a plan, and emphasize the importance of following directions, asking questions, and clear communication. Basic cooking skills were learned and reinforced. The rest of the family was responsible for doing the dishes and cleaning-up—another practical life lesson. As soon as dishes were done, we could proceed to the second part of Family Night—a fun activity.

One week we might go bowling or go on a bike ride; we might play board games or put a jig-saw puzzle together; or, we might pop popcorn and watch a rented movie of their choice.

After the activity, we started to wind the evening down, and transition to "Family Heart Talk." The night's leader got the family's "Talking Stick" from the cupboard where it laid in its own special spot. We made the stick on our very first Family Night. It was a one-inch diameter dowel rod and twelve inches long, that we sanded, painted, and decorated.

There was one steadfast rule for "Heart Talk" - you could only talk if you had the Talking Stick in your hand.

The leader would start. Taking turns, the person with the stick went around the circle, sharing with each person, one thing they liked and appreciated about that person and one thing they disagreed with or didn't appreciate. When the leader was done, the stick was passed to the person sitting next to them. No one could talk, interrupt, refute, comment, or reply when another person had the Talking Stick. We could respond to what someone said to us or about us *only* when it was our turn.

Wow! Bill and I learned *so* much. We took in the positive comments, as well as areas alerting us like flashing lights of items needing our immediate attention. Because of Family Night, we learned about bullying and things going on or issues the kids were scared or confused about (i.e. my cancer and surgeries). We were delighted when we heard many positive things in each other's' lives we might not have otherwise known.

Once a month, we added a "Family Favorite" question time to the end of the weekly Heart Talk. The question we added was, "Is there an activity we haven't done as a family you want to do?"

Because of the answers we heard, we ventured onto turf we, as parents, might never have thought of—like taking scuba diving lessons as a family, sleeping outside under the stars on our front lawn, or telling scary stories before drifting off to slumber. We even went on a midnight snow machine ride.

Family Night always closed in prayer—each person taking a turn praying. The leader opened and closed the night in prayer. The good-night hug often turned into a mock wrestling match, laughter and glee filling the air as "The Hulk" (Bill's college nickname) roared and picked up one child in each arm and take them to the bottom of the stairs leading up to their bedrooms.

The kids have told us instituting Family Night was pivotal as they grew up. While it was hard hearing discouraging, sometimes harsh words, it was equally nice hearing good things. It one of the best things we ever did as a family. Tools they used and lessons they learned from Family Night are now in their own adult tool-boxes. They have shared seeing the results of our prayers in action, and it has kept the communication lines between us open as well.

Family Night was a safe place for *all* of us. It was a place we could be real, open and honest, no matter what was going on. Family Night helped to prepare each of us for the time came for when the kids eventually left the nest. It let each family member vent in a safe environment. It aided Bill and me as we learned how to cope and deal with growing pains and new situations.

Family night helped all of us as we struggled and lived out being on what we called the medical mission field. Talking-Stick time assisted us as we learned to become better listeners. We gained new perspectives and insights, learning how to deal with our kid's individual physical and special needs. From genetic traits to abuse/neglect issues, the challenges of adoption, having autistic tendencies and cerebral palsy was a lot to deal with. Bill and I learned so much from them. And the kids learned Bill and I were *far* from perfect!

All for One ... and One for All.

32

I NEED A BREAK

Our first introduction to *Joni and Friends*™ was their Family Retreat in 1991. I had seen an intriguing brochure for the retreat at a book store and brought it home. It seemed exactly what our family could use at the time—and it didn't hurt that it was at one of our favorite beach towns on the Oregon Coast.

I brought the brochure home to Bill. He agreed it looked like a great retreat for our family, and sounded like a lot of fun. *But* summer is high season for those in the construction field. Try as he might, he couldn't arrange to take the time off—especially since he was the superintendent on the job, and they were on a on a tight deadline to complete the project on time.

Bill knew how much I wanted us to go as a full family. He came over and enveloped me in one his firm, loving, and humongous hugs. He said to me, "Why don't you take the kids and go have fun? It will be a good time. You need it."

While I was disappointed Bill couldn't get the time off, and I hated to go without him, I *was* excited for the retreat. I was once again amazed by my husband's sacrifice—I knew he wanted "family time," too.

With a smile, he added, "I think this is going to be one of those funny times God provides for *each* of us in ways we could never ask, think, or imagine.

We applied to attend and explained why Bill couldn't be there.

Despite the fact we weren't going as the whole family, we were accepted.

It was official. The kids and I were going.

The day finally came for us to leave for Family Retreat. Bill prayed over us as we hugged and said our tearful good-byes. I tooted the horn as we drove away, the kids waving until Dad was out of sight.

At the retreat center, we enjoyed five days filled with worship, teaching, and an amazing assortment of activities. We rubbed elbows with other families who understood the physical, emotional, spiritual, and financial challenges that are part of each day when a member is disabled and/or has special needs.

I was in a rare environment where I could be *me*. Just. Me.

I wasn't the occupational therapist. I wasn't the patient. I wasn't the mom with a child who has special needs. I was just plain Care.

For my entire life, I have lived with hidden disabilities. I live with my non-existent immune system, multiple orthopedic and neurological impairments, my brain injury, or cancer. My "normal" changes each and every day I wake up. At Family Retreat I found out it was the same for others. It was a comfort people not only understood it, they lived it, too. I was surrounded by new friends who gave me the gift of being listened to, encouraged, stretched, but more importantly accepted. Just the way I was.

During meals, free time, and especially during a daily group time for women, I talked with other women with disabilities and chatted with moms whose kid(s) or spouse had special needs. (The men had their own group.) I let down my protective guard without fear of being judged. I was among others who understood what it was like to daily, sometimes hourly, experience many of the same obstacles and adventures disability brought into our family life.

I found camaraderie with these people. They didn't run away when I had a complete toxic waste meltdown—crying and releasing years of pent-up tears and concerns about coping and living with issues of disability all while being a part of the medical profession. When I finished unloading my burdens and came to the end of myself, they prayed *for* me, and laughed *with* me. Not *at* me.

At Family Retreat our son was able to accept his special needs. He found out during the kids' activities time he was not alone. There were other kids who understood what it was like to feel lonely, isolated, or misunderstood because they were different.

There was special sibling time where our daughter was able to discover she wasn't the only one who had to deal on a day-to-day basis with life involving a family member who had a disability or special needs. She learned lessons of coping, communication, and compassion serving her well in the future.

During afternoon free time, we came back together as a family and enjoyed time at the shores of one of our favorite beaches. We played in the tide pools off Haystack Rock, ran in the surf, and collected shells to decorate the sandcastle we had made. One day we visited the local candy store where we watched bubble-gum flavored salt-water taffy being made and then enjoyed sampling it. YUM!

In the evening, everyone from the retreat gathered down at the beach. We sat or stood around a large, blazing campfire. We sang songs and roasted marshmallows for s'mores. The town had pulled out all the stops to make the beach as accessible as possible. Right down to a plywood ramp leading down to the beach so persons with mobility needs could participate in the campfire time. It was a first for many in wheelchairs to actually be *on* the sandy beach. What a thrill it was to watch their excitement as they wiggled toes in the sun-warmed sand or let the sand sift through their hands!

As I looked around the campfire, my heart was warmed. Not just by the campfire, but by the expressions on radiant faces reflecting sweet peace and contentment as they sang, chatted, roasted marshmallows, or indulged in the gooey sweet treat of a s'more.

As the evening stars began to twinkle, people shared how special and accepted they had felt the last five days at Family Retreat.

One young boy shared, "It's been cool not to be made fun of because I look different."

A mom, tears slipping down her cheeks said, "I was able to watch my daughter laugh and play games *for the very first time*, just like normal kids do!"

After clearing his throat several times, a dad piped up and revealed he had never had a chance to talk with other men about how they handled family-life and the financial challenges. It was a blessing to him to watch and be around other families who walked a similar path his family did.

Several families excitedly announced once they returned home, they were going to share stories with their friends, family, and churches what they had experienced and learned. They wanted others to know how important it is for *everyone*—including those affected by disability—to feel accepted and encouraged. The families wanted to share with people even though they might have a disability, they were still valuable, and *could* participate in normal activities.

Others shared their excitement to show people the resources as a way to help introduce others to the many ways they can practically reach out to the disabled and include them in *all* areas and aspects of church and community activities.

As the embers of the campfire began to die down, campers slowly made their way back to their rooms at the Conference Center. The embers may have started to die down, but I had a hunch the glow was going to linger and radiate in their lives for a long time.

The following day, the kids and I returned home to find not only the home fire burning, but a warm glow in Bill's eyes. God *had* shown up in ways I could never think, ask, or imagine. While the kids and I were filled to the brim from having fun, learning and growing, Bill had his *own* time of respite and renewal, learning and growing.

He shared he hadn't realized how much he needed the peace and quiet time away from *anything* resembling disability. He hadn't realized (nor had I, quite frankly) how burned out he had become being immersed in 24/7 disability ministry. He was the husband, the dad, the provider, and more. He was a caregiver and a "taker of Care." He was my rehab engineer/creative consultant when I needed help adapting equipment for me or my OT clients. He realized it was totally okay (and necessary) to take time off and get away, alone with God.

As our weary heads hit the pillow our first night home, Bill shared while we were at Family Retreat, he truly experienced what God meant to "*be still and know*" (Psalm 46:10 NLV) in the calm and quiet.

God had heard the unspoken cry of his burned-out heart, mind, and soul. He said he couldn't believe that before he had dared to even ask God for a time of respite, the Father had known his heart and lovingly answered in the way *only* He can.

What a mighty God we have. A God who takes each one of us, right where we are, and who answers our unspoken, sometimes unknown need. Family life, especially when one or more of the members has a disability, can be challenging—even on a good day.

Time for respite and renewal and time to be still and listen, are important coping skills we learned to build into our family because of Family Retreat.

How long has it been since you took some time to "be still and know?"

33

I WISH TIME WAS EXTINCT

After all the therapy from the car accident and the total knee surgery, I knew going back to work as an occupational therapist was a lofty goal to work toward. I continued to look for ways to reclaim some normalcy to my days, so just *maybe* I could return to work. Coaching the local swim team and picking up the kids from school were starting points, to be sure.

One day, while waiting in the elementary school car-pool-pick-up line, I tapped my fingers on the steering wheel, getting lost in time to the tunes of one of my favorite worship songs on the radio.

Exactly at 3:22, bouncing bundles of energy burst through the large, metal front doors of the school. Twinkling eyes scanned the horizon for their family's vehicle in the pick-up line. Kids (mine included!) leaping and bouncing like jumping beans across the road to where parents—often impatiently—waited for the other urchins and their parents to move out of the long, congested, loading zone.

I urged my kids to jump into the car quickly. Once the kids rambunctiously clambered in, and secured their seatbelts, we were off.

When we arrived home, the kids quickly unbuckled their seat belts, slammed the car doors and ran like lightning into the house. By the time I brought up the rear and entered the house, the kids were rifling through the snack cupboard and refrigerator.

I admonished them to save room for dinner. They rolled their eyes at me.

They moaned and groaned, declaring: "Mom! We're *starving...*"

"Well make it snappy—you have chores to get to," I responded, using my "tired mom" voice they knew all too well.

While they continued to forage, I checked the telephone answering machine.

Finding no messages to attend to I refocused my attention to the kids. I hadn't noticed while I was checking for phone messages, they had finished their snack and were taking turns using the bathroom.

I knew we were on a tight time schedule—especially if I were to get them to our church's scouting program on time. I started barking like a drill sergeant: "Hustle, Hustle! You have chores to do! Hustle!"

I hollered at Jamie to hurry up and get her piano practicing done. She was working on a piece of sheet music I thought should be easy for her. In my frustration, I barked out timing sequences, and clapped my hands loudly for emphasis. She stopped and started over and over again, making more mistakes instead of less.

A twinge of guilt washed over me. It wasn't fair to her as I became conscious I was verbally taking out *my* stress on *her.* She was practicing diligently. I realized her starting over multiple times was her way of seeking to please me and gain my approval. I felt like a failure as a mom.

If things weren't bad enough barking like I drill sergeant as Jamie practiced piano, I heard my *other* child upstairs playing with Legos™ instead of finishing his chores."

I roared at my son: "You have five minutes, mister, to pick up your toys, get your scouting gear and get into to the car."

I heard a CA-THUMP, BUMP, BUMP sound coming from

his room.

"What are you DOING?" I shrieked at my Lego™-loving son.

"*Nothing*, Mom!" Tim hollered back down to me.

I knew *exactly* what *that* "nothing" meant. I could feel myself beginning to steam, my vent was about to blow.

My drill sergeant tone of voice boomed, "*Get in the car – NOW!*"

I took in a deep breath, double checked on the crock-pot stew cooking for dinner, and made sure we all had the items needed for Scouts.

As we roared off to Scouts, I found myself going over the posted speed limit. I was distracted by a not-so-quiet, (supposed to be whispered) conversation between the kids in the back-seat.

My son whispered, "In circle time today we talked about stuff that bugs us. Then we had to write about it."

His sister asked him what he wrote.

I wrote: "I wish time was extinct like dinosaurs so my family wasn't always in a hurry."

I glanced in the rear view mirror just in time to see Jamie nod her head in agreement. I wanted to die a thousand deaths with what I overheard. It was true. It *does* often feel like we are dragging the kids through life as if they were a dog on a leash. We rush through after school snacks and dinner; then homework, and necessary chores; then it's off to church, Scouts, choir or some other function.

Some great mother I am, I lamented.

Once we got home from Scouts, ate dinner, made one last check to make sure the kids' homework was done and showers taken, Bill and I scooted them off to bed. We joined with them in their bedtime prayers.

Wearily following Bill down the stairs after tucking them in, I went in and collapsed on our bed. I was past being exhausted.

I looked up to Heaven and whispered, "God, *I* wish time was extinct, too."

My whispered prayer was abruptly interrupted by a gentle knock on the door.

"Mom, can I come in?" Jamie's voice was muffled through the closed door.

"Sure, sweetie, but aren't you supposed to be in bed, asleep?" I quickly sat myself upright.

She slowly opened the door and climbed up on the bed responding, "Yes, but we were so busy earlier today I forgot to tell you something really, really important happened. Remember my unfinished, school essay assignment you and dad grounded me for until I got it done??"

My cheeks flushed a hot pink.

Sheepishly I looked at Jamie and said "How could I forget? We went around and around about the assignment. It was *not* optional. And yes, you *did* get grounded."

"Well…guess what, mom? My teacher entered it into a contest and I won 2nd place in the *whole* county and I won a $50 savings bond! And they are going to use the picture I drew and put it on t-shirts, tote-bags, hats and aprons for a fund raiser—for a whole *YEAR*! The money will go for stuff to help kids who are abused. Isn't that cool?

Then she asked, "Wanna read it? You never got to see it finished. *Puleeze*, Mom?"

Waiting for me to reply, she started jumping up and down on our bed.

I felt ashamed, knowing the type of day we had all endured. I wasn't sure I was prepared for she wrote. The unintentionally overheard, not-so-quietly whispered conversation about wishing time were extinct had pierced me to the core. I was afraid of what an entire paragraph might do to me.

I responded (more from my shame and feeling like I was miserable mother) saying, "Well, sweetie, why don't *you* read it? They're *your* words."

"Okay!" She beamed. "Ready?" she asked, taking one last jump, landing her bottom firmly on the bed.

"Here goes!" she said with a grin displaying her missing teeth. It's called "*What My Home Means to Me.*"

"*My home is a fun place to be. It is full of love and fun people. It is full of nice and neatness. We hike on our hill and have lots of family time. I love my home and the people who live in it. It is like a quilt of many colors wrapped in love.*"

Tears slipped down my cheeks.

"Why are you crying, Mom? Aren't you proud of me?" Jamie asked with a concerned look on her sweet face.

I assured her I was indeed proud of her. I swept her up in a big hug and smothered her with hugs. I explained my tears were happy tears. They were tears of gratitude and relief, and maybe, just maybe, I wasn't a failure as a mom.

"Don't worry, Mom. We all have those kinds of days!" She said, drying my tears with her nightgown sleeve.

As she bounded out of the room, she looked back and said, "And Mom? You're *not* a failure. You're a great mom…*my* mom!" And with that she ambled off to bed.

Oh… out of the mouth of babes.

I'm sure glad God works through us even when we feel like we are a failure. I'm glad, too, that our kids loved us in spite of ourselves, even when they (and we?) wish time were extinct.

I shot a glance upwards and whispered, "*Thank You, Lord, for loving us even when we stumble; for always there to catch us and carry us through. Thank You for the life lessons I am learning,—especially reminding me to keep my priorities straight and to stay within the boundaries You have set for me. Help me point others to You.*

Help me to look for the silver linings in the storm clouds that blow through my life, and to always look to You for strength for the day — even on the days when I, too, wish time was extinct."

How do *you* respond on the days you might wish time were extinct?

34

IN THE PITS

Our family pace eased into a comfortable routine, at least for us. After completing several union carpentry jobs, Bill took a break to help a friend who owned a rock drilling business. It was a welcome breather and a new venture for him. He delighted in learning the drilling business—working with different types of heavy equipment and the opportunity to acquire additional skills.

The men left in the wee hours of the morning, driving to remote logging sites or rock pits. They spent long hours drilling and blasting rock, often returning home after dark. Some evenings Bill came home so covered in black grime, grease and grit, I could barely tell him apart from the dark night—until he flashed his pearly whites in a tired but happy camper smile (especially on "blast" days!) Oh, our men with their big-boy toys! He thoroughly enjoyed the friendship, fellowship, and working camaraderie as he worked side by side with his friend. It was a win-win experience.

Bill and I often joked we should change our names to Fred and Wilma, like the characters in the *Flintstones*™ cartoon. It would be fitting as Bill was working in rock quarries, while my body was a (human) rock quarry as my litany of surgeries continued.

While Bill used construction grade drills, jack-hammers, and tools to dynamite rock for new projects or reconstructed roads, my surgeons used their surgical grade drills, jack-hammers, and medical tools to blast different parts of my body, reconstructing and repairing what they could.

One night I told Bill, "I am so tired of being in the pits. I was weary of being in a never-ending state of surgery and rehabilitation. I was drained from the relentless regime of my body being under construction, reconstruction, or restoration—not to mention being in constant pain.

Every fiber of my being—physical, emotional, and spiritual had been hammered at. It left me feeling shattered to bits. I felt disfigured from the multiple surgeries. When I ran my fingers over my incisions, the texture resembled the bumpy logging roads we drove over. "Some poor soul will need a map to figure out which incision scar leads to where, after I die. I've gone from being a strong boulder to a fragmented pebble of who I physically used to be." I commiserated to Bill.

He shook his head and gave me one of his piercing looks. "You are beautiful inside and out. You may be a smaller version of yourself, physically, and permanently weaker, but you need to remember: when *you* are at your weariest and weakest from being drilled upon, those are the times when God uses what you have gone through to make you stronger and better. Being dynamited is a *good* thing!"

I leaned back and took a deep breath. "Like being pruned, huh?"

He took my hand and squeezed. "Think about it this way: Rocks come in various sizes, shapes and colors, and are used for a variety of purposes. Some large, over-size boulders are so big they are meant to be left in place, to stabilize a riverbed or protect the area around it. Other boulders are out of man's reach and will be left in a riverbed where water vibrantly cascades and pounds over them. The rock shimmers in the bright sunlight, sunbeams reflecting heavenly glory.

"Other times, a large boulder is drilled and blasted into smaller pieces, to be used for a variety of things. Some of the rock we drill and blast will be brutally scraped and scooped up and fashioned into miles of new roads and trails—where it was once unbeaten paths. You are being blasted for a variety of uses, too, and taking a journey on new paths and roads you've never been on."

"But there are times I wish it could be an easier path – or at least a smoother one." I let out a long sigh.

Bill replied, "Don't lose sight that like the purpose for the rocks, you have great purpose too. Even if it's just to be used like the smaller rocks we use on a daily basis for making a driveway, landscaping projects or rock climbing walls. Some rocks will be piled for later use. The purpose for each rock—large or small, boulder or pebble—will be revealed in due time. But the rock *is* drilled for a purpose."

His words sank deep into my heart. Bill was never one to mince words. Honestly, I needed to hear it. No matter how difficult.

"Think about it, Care. Every surgery you have gone through, every procedure you have endured, God has used to be an encouraging 'at the end of your hand' moment. You have been able to help countless others. You are rock solid in your faith. His purpose *will* continue to be shown as you live out the life He has purposed for you—and *us*. We just have to continue to be willing to be used for His purpose, even if we get weary and worn."

I nodded because words were too hard to come by. I had been weary. And I was more than a little worn.

Bill stood, kissed my forehead and left to hit the sack a bit early. I sat in my recliner mulling over what he had said.

I let out another long breath. I looked upward and told the Master Craftsman and Superintendent of my Pit (God), "I am weary, I am worn, but I am willing to do my utmost best to use the lessons I learn while I'm in my quarry. Not just for me, but for whomever You send me at the end of my hand."

As I look back on that night, I realized I am still very much in my quarry. I am not finished being hammered on, drilled, or blasted by any stretch of *anyone's* imagination. I'm sure I will continue to sport many jagged cliffs in my quarry. There will be some steep, rugged rock walls to climb, not to mention some deep cavernous pits I'll probably slip and possibly fall into from time to time.

If my past is preparing me for the future, I know more conflicts, storms, and adventures will follow in the days ahead… and God has a plan for each one of them. Even when find myself in the pits.

35

HEARING VERSUS LISTENING

After four years, the hours and days of drilling rock became longer and longer. Sometimes jobs required Bill to be gone for days at a time. The kids missed their dad terribly. We did the best we could to juggle schedules to maximize what short time we had with him on days he was home.

Occasionally, during school breaks or at the height of the summer season when the job required seven days a week, dawn to dusk hours, we ventured to join the crew, setting up camp near the job site. Bill removed two of the three passenger bench seats of Old Blue—our passenger van—and turned it into a temporary mobile home.

Heart pounding wildly, I drove Old Blue up steep, often narrow, winding, rough logging roads. The kids laughed at me as I let out a shriek now and then. To them it was an adventure, but to me? I was sure at any moment, as we came around a sharp curve or I hit an unseen pothole we'd be sent tumbling over the steep edge, landing in the thick brush.

Scouting out possible camp sites in what seemed to be the middle of nowhere, we each had our specifications. Peace was reached when all (or most) site prerequisites were met. The kids wanted a place near a creek to play in. I wanted to be close to the drill site, yet far enough away to be safe and *not* hear the drone and noise of the equipment. Sunshine to bask in and *no* swarms of bees or mosquitos were certainly a bonus!

On one of camping trips, we got settled in our spot and I fixed lunch for the kids. Afterwards, they sped off to an adventure in the woods while I sat dangling my feet in the creek's cool water. It was a warm summer day and I lazily let my mind wander. My thoughts landed on how hard and long so many people worked on these types of jobs every day. Here I was doing nothing, while others were toiling miles away from civilization. The commitment of time, resources, and hard labor it took for rock drillers, heavy equipment operators, and forestry personnel, was immense.

Those long hours and days spent away from family were causing Bill to stretch the limits of our "family first" tenet, priority, and boundary. He missed us terribly. Work kept up at a steady pace, meaning continued time away. He *loved* what he was doing and his incredible boss. The finances were more than meeting our needs. But… his kids, approaching their teen years, were beckoning and begging him to be home more. A rare request he knew he needed to heed.

Driving home from camping near a job site in Old Blue late one Sunday afternoon, our daughter said, "Daddy…I wish you were still doing carpentry. Then we'd get to see you more."

He knew he had an excruciating but heart-right decision to make. He made the decision to quit. He may not know where or when his next paycheck came from, yet he knew one can't put a monetary price put on the rewards of being at home more to sow into the lives of his kids.

He sorely missed his time in the woods and rustic terrain. He missed the hard rock (literally!) and the grit and grime. He missed the fellowship of a good friend/boss, not to mention their favorite family-owned diner—Clark's.

When they drove the back road highway, if Clark's diner's light atop the telephone pole was on, it was a guaranteed stop.

They couldn't resist the one-pound homemade hamburger, piled high with all the fixings. It came with a pound of homemade, hand-cut crinkle French fries. To top the meal all off was an old-fashioned, *humongous* chocolate/peanut butter and banana milk shake topped with an ice cream sundae with whipped cream and a cherry on top, served in 1950-era metal, twenty-ounce milkshake cup.

We have learned (often by the school of hard knocks) that *listening* is equally, if not sometimes even more important than *hearing*. Bill had heard the cries and desires of our kids' hearts loud and clear. As head of our family, he knew the importance of leading by example. He wanted to model for the kids he had not only *heard* them, but he was *listening*. They were asking him to stay within the family boundaries and to keep his priorities straight. They were asking him to walk his talk of "faith and family first."

Love is often spelled T.I.M.E.

Boulders and bodies drilled and blasted, dirt, grime and gravel put aside, as a family there were new roads to travel upon and new experiences lay ahead.

Changing jobs, especially if it is a choice *you* make, is not always easy. It took Bill a lot of courage to man-up, realizing he had strayed from set priorities and boundaries as father and husband. And he was willing to admit it and make the necessary changes.

Courage to make changes may be challenging, but with faith covering your back, and when you hold to your priorities and boundaries, victory is not far behind.

Just ask Bill.

36

CAST IN CONCRETE

It took Bill a bit of time to catch up on missed sleep and unattended items on his honey-do list once his rock drilling days were over. He wasn't sure what he wanted to do job-wise, but knew he needed a job that provided good medical insurance and wages. Keeping up with my continued medical bills in addition to mounting grocery and clothing bills with two teens who had voracious appetites and seemingly hollow legs wasn't easy.

Bill decided to apply for work through the local area carpentry union. He knew if he got a call to work, the union had great wages and a generous benefit package. To his surprise, there was plenty of local work and the union called him within days of signing up.

The variety of union jobs Bill worked allowed him to continue enhancing his professional skills and resume. He gained the nickname, "Mr. Concrete" as he became adept at pouring and assembling new concrete tilt walls at a frozen food facility. He literally climbed to new heights as he worked on the looming stacks at a regional steam plant. Bill's construction proficiency on multiple levels added to his gifts of common-sense problem solving. His real and clear communication with co-workers, led him to a supervisory role on more than one job. Supervisors and union officials were impressed and took note. As one union job ended, another shortly became available.

One of Bill's favorite union jobs was the new construction of a local area high school. The job brought out the best in Bill—his creativity, his ability to work with not just carpentry laborers, but electricians, plumbers, landscapers and more. It took more than a village to build the new, state-of-the-art high school.

As the school neared completion, several area contractors and union officials recognized Bill's concrete, construction, and collaborative skills. They offered him a promotion on an up-coming contract. The job was building the new hydroelectric dam in the eastern part of the county. It was a job requiring the type of precision concrete skills Bill had.

The bad news was it meant a 45-minute commute from home. Bill told the union officials he was elated to be considered, but the decision to accept the esteemed promotion needed to be a *family* decision. We learned later his decision statement earned Bill even more respect with the union officials.

Driving home after the offer, Bill was deep in thought, reminiscing how he had finished the carport and shop just the way he wanted it. He recalled the many hours of H-O-R-S-E played on the multi-purpose concrete floor carport and basketball half-court with the kids and teen youth group. He thought about the many hours and deep conversations we had while soaking in the hot tub. He had *finally* laid the carpet—just two months prior to the offer. The log house was the longest we had lived in one place since we'd been married. Ten years in one place was a monumental accomplishment for us!

When he got home, Bill called a family meeting. Sitting around the kitchen table, he shared the job opportunity offered to him, including the part about telling the powers that be the decision would be a *family* decision – including Aunt Betty, since the decision affected her as well.

We started the decision-making process by creating a family pro and con list. We told the kids to think hard about all the activities they were involved in—our church's youth group, soccer, scouting, and music lessons. If we were to continue with our professed family values, priorities, and boundaries, it meant driving time and activities had to be kept to a minimum. We bantered back and forth, crossed some things off, moving other items to the opposite column.

The tone of voices grew loud and testy as we attempted to talk over each other. Wisely, Bill called for a fifteen minute time-out so we could stretch our legs, breathe, and refuel with a quick snack. He told us to step outside, take in four deep breaths of fresh air, hold it to the count of seven, and then slowly let the breath out to the count of eight. Then repeat it three times.

We call it the "4-7-8" tool from our family toolbox. It is used to clear our heads and thought processes. (And is great when your mind is racing and you can't fall asleep at night. Try it for yourself sometime!)

Fifteen minutes later, we returned for one last look at the list we had compiled.

We were ready to vote. A secret ballot was taken. It was a unanimous decision. The aye's had it—even with the one caveat placed *before* we voted. The caveat? It meant a move to keep the commute to a minimum. Apparently, everyone agreed it was doable—even Aunt Betty sharing she was up for one more move and adventure.

Bill returned to work the next day, telling union officials he was willing to accept the job as the night shift supervisor, overseeing the new construction of the new dam.

Apparently, we'd set a tradition with our first home and carpeting. I hoped it didn't mean we'd *never* get to live in a house with newly laid carpet on the floor for more than two months.

37

MOVING AND MORE

It was pretty evident this move had some advanced "Providential Project Planning," as the details and timing all came together within weeks of our decision. The log house sold in a short week of our decision. A couple in our church heard we were going to put the house on the market. Ironically, they had looked at the house before we bought it. Ten years earlier, they were ready to put an offer on the fixer-upper, only to hear it had sold to us. They told us later we made almost the *exact* same remodeling decisions they had wanted to make—right down to the paint scheme and furniture arrangement. Talk about being reminded The Master Carpenter was into details!

Selling the house allowed us to keep within our family boundary with commute time and still be centralized to accommodate everyone's activities. We found a three-bedroom house with an enclosed detached shop/garage, ready to be moved into right away

There was an added bonus of a small one-bedroom mother-in-law house, perfect for Aunt Betty. She was elated to have her own place and live rent free. I made sure she didn't miss out on her girls' day out or special senior adult church activities at our former church.

I had recently returned to work part-time as an itinerant rural school occupational therapist for the county Educational School District. At the time, I was assigned to three rural schools closest to our home. It was great as I had the same schedule as the kids and could still juggle their after-school activities and still coach the age-group swim team. With the move though, I reluctantly had to resign as the swim team coach.

Once we moved, I was able to negotiate with my boss to switch which rural schools I covered. Once again, God went before me. When I approached my employer to ask about switching schools, he told me the OT who had been covering the three school districts nearest to our new home, wanted to switch to the schools *I* had been covering.

*God*incidence!

Each school was within twenty minutes of our new home. Bill had a ten-minute commute to his new work site. It was the first (and only) time we lived in a neighborhood where homes were close to each other—like hear the neighbors' conversations close.

The kids walked six blocks to their schools. We lived two blocks from the local hospital and five blocks from the local grocery store. For the first time, our kids lived where there were paved roads perfect to ride bikes and skateboard on.

The kids easily made new friends at school. While the tiny town population of 1,000 was much smaller than the town we moved from (population 17,000) the school division sports league were still the same. To their delight, they were able to see their friends frequently as they participated in or went to sporting events.

Bill's union wages, added to my part-time income working as a school OT, afforded us our first opportunity to allow ourselves *not* to adhere to the time-honored *Lesson of the Ring*. The decision resulted in a want vs. true need purchase—a new sixteen-foot pleasure boat. With Bill working nights, we had afternoons, early evenings, and many weekends to spend on the water.

The east end of the county had several lakes and rivers in close proximity to our house. Many were a short ten to fifteen minute drive away. It was not hard to get our teen and pre-teen to spend time with us, their *old* (to them) parents. With Bill working the night shift, we were able to spend many afternoon hours and lazy weekend days inner-tubing, water skiing, and just plain relaxing, soaking up the sun, spending time as a family together.

Aunt Betty had never been on a personal boat ride. She delighted in the beauty of God's creation as we discovered hidden bays, watched birds and wildlife not seen in a town or city. She especially enjoyed the times where we were able to get within a mile of the construction site, marveling at the progress being made. We never could get her to go inner-tubing, but she *loved* going fast with the water spraying over the bow!

Two years flew by. Before we knew it, Bill's job was finishing up, even though a partial remodel of our house was *not*. (Did you *really* think I could keep the temptation of remodeling *some*thing in the house from a die-hard carpenter? Um… no.)

On the Thursday of the final week of the project, a public ceremony and viewing of the dam was held. The company that held the contract awarded Bill a commemorative gold belt buckle with an etching of the dam. They recognized Bill's expertise, his diversified skills, and his no-nonsense and (not so common) common sense style helped the job to be completed early. The combination of Bill's attributes and actions resulted in not only saving the county money, but a nice bonus for the contractor and kudos to the local union.

After the recognition ceremony and local newspaper photo-ops were complete, several union officials took Bill aside. They thanked him again and then turned the conversation over to union officials and contractors from the opposite side of the state. These officials came not only for the ceremony, but to meet the infamous "Mr. Concrete" in person.

Unbeknownst to Bill, reports of his expertise, abilities, and knowledge working with concrete had spread. The officials and contractors had talked to his current supervisors, inquiring if they thought Bill might be willing to relocate to the eastern part of the state.

A major project, involving concrete expertise, carpentry, and the ability to think-outside-the-box was in the planning stage. The officials, liking what they had seen first-hand and the multiple commendations given at the ceremony, they asked Bill if he might like to be a part of the up-coming project. The job was located at a rural dam, and the officials knew if Bill was there, he could handle any problems that might arise.

A deluge of rain began, so the discussion moved inside—to the trailer doubling as the project office. Officials shared more in-depth details about the project and ended the hour-long discussion by offering Bill a handsome financial and benefit package. For planning purposes, the officials needed Bill's decision by Monday morning.

Bill came home, exhausted. He had worked his twelve-hour night-shift, plus an additional four hours for the ceremony and photo-ops, then the discussion with the union officials. His mind was reeling. He shared with me the short version of the conversation and the offer they had made. He told me he didn't have a clue what to do, other than pray…hard.

I told him to sleep on it and we'd talk after he was more rested and could think more clearly.

Sometimes, all we need to do is: Stop; Drop; Rest; And Pray… *before* we cast our nets.

38

CASTING OUT OUR NET OF FAITH

Bill had been looking forward to the job being completed so he could return to working during the day shift, not nights. He wanted to take some time off in between jobs to finish the partial remodel of our house. But now everything was up in the air.

The sheetrock was up and fresh paint applied. New cabinets were hung in the kitchen and new counter-tops installed. The carpet had been picked out and ordered, just not laid. The carpet had arrived several weeks earlier than scheduled, so the multiple rolls of carpet and padding were relegated to being stored in the garage.

Bill's mind was not the only one reeling. His news had set *my* mind reeling. Leaning on some of the common sense decision making skills I had gleaned from being married to Bill, I started with prayer for wisdom, discernment, and above all, peace. I was fresh and ready for whatever the day brought on.

After thinking about our conversation about the new offer, I picked up my Occupational Therapy Association's phone directory and the recent newsletter. I started scanning the section for the eastern part of the state. I found several intriguing jobs, but two really jumped out. One was working for a rural home health agency, the other for an itinerant rural school OT position. My inquiring mind let my fingers do the walking and my mouth did the talking.

When I made the first phone call, I was not expecting to get the Director of Special Services for rural schools. She introduced herself, and then said, "I'm not sure how you got connected to my extension, but I sure am glad you did!"

The rural service area was in *desperate* need of an occupational therapist. She needed an itinerant OT who didn't mind driving, who liked rural schools, and could interact with teachers, students, and families who lived in small, usually farming towns. The job was for three days a week, but ten to twelve hours with travel. The pay was almost double of a regular OT, plus they paid mileage and per diem. The territory covered a total of twenty-three school districts, spanning twenty to almost two hundred miles in-between. After verbally sharing my resume with her and what amounted to an unsolicited impromptu job interview, she asked if I meet her the following afternoon for a more formal interview. I'm not sure what prompted me, (it was a about a three hundred mile drive) other than the still small voice of the Holy Spirit, but I responded, "I'll be there."

Imagine Bill's surprise when he got up later in the afternoon and I sheepishly asked him if he could possibly miss the last day of work at the dam.

"Miss work? Why? What did you do?" His questions popped out at me like hot popcorn without a lid on it.

I explained it wasn't my intention to set up an interview, but when I made some calls just to see what *might* be available for me in the area, *just in case* we decided to move to take the union job, well, it just happened. I promised him I was only testing the waters, nothing was cast in concrete… yet.

Once the kids got home from school a family meeting was called—including Aunt Betty. The looks on their faces said it all: "*Uh-oh, here we go again!*"

Bill shared the offer with them, and then I shared my conversation and upcoming interview.

Without a word, our son went and got a sheet of paper and made two columns. The drill from two years prior was still fresh in his mind. We started making the pros and cons list.

Again.

But this time, much more was at stake. It required a five to six-hour move, not a forty-five minute commute. We were unfamiliar with the eastern part of the state, save the week-long swim camp I had coached at a college in 1989, and Bill driving a truck hauling hay in the mid-late 1970's. Yes, we had visited Bill's folks when they were camping at Soap Lake, but that was only half-way across the state.

The peppering questions began. Do we have to sell the house? Does it mean we will have to move? We won't have to sell the boat, will we? If we have to move, will Aunt Betty come with us?

School-wise, the timing for both kids couldn't be more ideal. One was headed into middle-school and the other into high school once school was out for the summer, in three weeks. Voice decibels began to rise. Bill called for a time out and tabled the discussion until after dinner so we could each clear our heads and think more about it. As we dispersed, I reminded them that either way, I was leaving early the next morning to drive to the area for an interview.

Bill called his supervisor at the project, asking if he was really needed for the last night. He explained about my calling about OT jobs in the eastern part of the state, and had an interview the next day.

His supervisor had been at the previous day's meeting and aware of the union official's conversation with him earlier. "You'd be a fool to show up tonight. All we have to do is a last bit of clean-up from the public ceremony and a crew party afterward—and I know how much you *love* the kind of partying *these* guys do!" as he chuckled.

"Not!" Bill replied with his signature laugh. "As long as you give me the okay it is not a big deal, I'd like to go check things out."

His supervisor told him, "I bet you could probably get paid for the trip—just stop in at the Union Hall, and ask for who you met. You'll blow them out of the water!"

So after dinner and a little more discussion, the ballots were passed out. The results were tallied. The ayes had it, but with one abstention: Aunt Betty. She said she needed more time to think about if she wanted to move and start all over again.

Bill looked at the ballots and announced, "Well, it looks like we have our third almost-laid-carpet-call. Mom and I will go check out the area tomorrow and we might even stay the weekend—that is, if we can trust the three of *you* to not party-hearty while we're gone."

Aunt Betty let out her one of her signature, mischievous giggles and said, "Oh, we'll party alright! TV Dinners™ and Oreos™ are on me, kiddos!"

Good ol' Oreos™ and TV Dinners™ of mac and cheese. If only all our decisions in life could bring such comfort. It was a good reminder of one of my favorite sayings from Corrie Ten Boom: "*Never be afraid to trust an unknown future to a known God.*"

39

WHEN UNEXPECTED BECOMES REAL

As it turned out, God *had* gone well ahead of us, paving the way for new opportunities and adventures. We should have known He had, because He always did.

By the sheer numbers of God-winks and *God*incidences we encountered over the next few days, it was clear the move to the eastern part of the state was on the way to becoming a reality—much sooner than we anticipated.

During the formal interview on Friday, I was offered and accepted, the OT position as an itinerant, school-based occupational therapist. The job started in two weeks.

Bill's impromptu stop at the union hall *did* surprise the people who had spoken to him just two days earlier. Yet the look on their faces told Bill something was different. The union officials shared when they returned, the project they wanted Bill on had been delayed. They weren't sure how long the project delay might be; only the decision was in the hands of State and Federal officials, not the unions'.

But, they *did* guarantee Bill work on whatever union projects were going at the time. The officials told Bill they could find other local union carpentry jobs if he was still willing to make the move. Bill assured them he was willing to move– and to work, but asked for a month's time off to tackle all the details of moving. For good measure, he asked the union officials to put their words in writing, to legally protect all parties involved.

After our meetings, Bill and I called Aunt Betty to check in. She assured us things were under control and they were having a ball. Aunt Betty encouraged us to go ahead and stay the weekend. We took her up on her offer, knowing neighbors and friends were close by if extra help was needed.

We used our rare date time Friday afternoon and evening, to drive around and check the region out. We enjoyed seeing the sights and discovering opportunities available to us as a family. We also used the time to look at housing options. For the time being, we decided to look for a month-to-month rental home, as we didn't know how long it might take for our current house to sell.

We knew we didn't want to live in the city. We are *not* city-dwellers! Knowing my job involved travel around the eastern part of the state, we looked for a semi-centralized area. We poured over several real estate publications and the area newspaper's "Homes to Rent" section. After perusing papers, we moseyed about, driving an hour north of my job headquarters, into more rural areas.

On Saturday, we spent most of the day meeting with owners, managers, and real estate agents, looking for a place we felt fit our needs. As evening fell, we returned to our hotel. We were disheartened after eight hours of driving around, trekking over many properties, and viewing several homes; we had not found anything to our liking. We were anxious to find *something* before we left the area Sunday afternoon.

Dejected, we decided a long overdue special date night might help put things in perspective. It had been ages since we had eaten out without kids and/or Aunt Betty in tow. We chose a fine dining restaurant whose glossy brochure touted the best of the best, overlooking a spectacular waterfall. To my delight, we were seated at a table next to a cozy fireplace and had a stunning view of the waterfall.

It was a perfect atmosphere to continue our conversation about our hopes and dreams, and where we felt God was leading us. We talked at length as we dined over a scrumptious steak dinner. Neither Bill nor I had a peace about properties or options we had seen so far.

As we indulged with an enormous slice of Mississippi Mud Pie, we decided to set out early Sunday morning, on our own. We decided to head again in a northerly direction, asking God to guide us to where He wanted us to land.

40

WHAT IN THE WORLD JUST HAPPENED?

Our early morning journey led us to a small town, once a boomtown. We picked up a copy of their local monthly paper. It was a true country type newspaper. The paper featured ads and blurbs about upcoming area events, with the remaining ten or so pages filled with articles written by locals – regaling stories of days gone by and the latest news and accolades of current area residents.

During the early 1900's, the town once boasted a state-of-the-art hospital, a mercantile, railroad station, and school. Now, the cemetery, the VFW Hall, post office, a smaller version of the mercantile, and the dilapidated remnants of the original school, plus a beautiful hand-carved "Welcome" sign hung remained of the once boom town square.

Driving back roads, we saw a "For Sale by Owner" sign in front of an empty house on ten acres. It had a full view of the north side of a mountain. Our interest was piqued. We called the number on the sign. The owners were more than happy to show us the house, and could meet us there in a half hour.

As Bill and I sat waiting on firm, *straight* concrete porch steps, looking at the mountain, one of our favorite life sayings came to mind: "*Go up to the mountains, bearer of Good News; Say to the peoples: Here is Your God.*"

I mused, "First we lived at the literal foothills of Mt. Rainier, and then Mount St. Helens and the eruption...will *this* be the third mountain we are to 'go up to?'"

In the distance we heard the unmistakable sound of a motorcycle. To our surprise, a motorcycle drove up the circular gravel driveway. A woman nimbly climbed off the hog – she appeared to be in her seventies. She was followed by her husband, who sported a baseball cap with an imitation long pony-tail sticking out the back. We knew from the moment they greeted us, this was going to be no ordinary encounter. The introduced themselves, "Just call us Reka and Tony. Or 'hey you,' whichever you prefer!"

We found out the house was part of Reka's long-held family homestead farm. (Score one for farm-boy-Bill's vote.) It was the *only* parcel separated from the original homestead. We were dismayed to find out the large, faded, and weather-worn wooden barn was not part of the property. The barn had been in the family for generations, and the seller's daughter and family, who lived next door wanted to continue the tradition.

Reka chattered away as we toured the two-story with daylight basement. It had four bedrooms and two bathrooms. Reka continued regaling stories of past memories she and her family had made while they lived there. A cozy living room with a brick fireplace warmed them on cold snowy days and nights; a large laundry area and family room downstairs were in constant use.

Sitting on ten acres, with a small creek running on the property line, the home held memories of bringing friends and family together for many good times, Reka reminisced. The kitchen and dining area had large windows that looked out over the property, including the full view of Mount Spokane.

Reka stared at the mountain. "This house holds family memories close to my heart. I don't want this house to go to just *any*body. I know God will show me who is supposed to have it. I've had offers made—even higher than what I am asking. But the sale of this house isn't about money. This sale is a sale of my heart."

Reka and I sat down on a sofa in the living area and chatted, getting to know each other a bit. When I asked why she was selling the home, she told me it had been her home with her first husband—the first modern home on the homestead. Then her husband got cancer. She nursed him before he passed away from a long, hard battle, five years prior. As a single tear rolled down her cheek, I grabbed her hands in mine and shared with her some of my battles with cancer.

I told Reka about the life saying that had come to mind when I looked at the top of the mountain while we waited for them to arrive. She looked at me and brought her hands up to her mouth.

Several more tears slipped down her rose-tinted cheeks. "There were many sleepless nights when I was caring for Dick. Weary, I'd come here, make a cup of tea and sit here on the couch, looking up at the beacon on top of the mountain and recite Psalm 121:1-2a '*I lift up my eyes to the hills. From where does my help come? My help comes from the Lord…*' (ESV) It was the only thing that got me through."

After several moments of silence, she continued with a smile, "Now, I am remarried, and God told me it was time to turn the house over to someone else. Someone He had in mind, and I think you and Bill are it."

I told her we felt the extraordinary and deep love as we walked through the house. Tangible marks like when we saw two generations' growth chart penciled in with dates and names on one of the door posts was one of them. In my heart, I wished this could be the house for us, but when she told me the price, my heart sank. Unfortunately, it was well over our budgeted range.

When I told her it was over our price range, I tried to paste on a smile and let her know how much we appreciated them showing us around. Reka asked me about our price range, but I couldn't tell her.

I *did* tell her until our house sold, we were actually looking for a house to rent, month-to-month, as we promised ourselves not to get in over our heads in debt. Nevertheless, we had been drawn to this place, even if just to look. We were sorry, but we couldn't take the house.

She snorted and smirked, "I'll be the one to decide *that*, missy!"

It was clear that I was well out of my league dealing with this spunky, four-foot-*maybe*-eleven-inch, gray haired, spit-fire of a woman.

Reka hollered to the men. She barked the order in a way the men *knew* they must heed it, on the double. Once the men joined us, Reka told us all she had made up her mind. Bill and I *were* going to buy the house, and there was no two ways about it.

She said, "Arguing with me is like arguing with God—you never win—so get in your car and follow us to the local diner. We are going to write up a real estate contract over a good old breakfast of biscuits and gravy. And there will be no arguing over the bill. It's ours."

Bill shot me a quizzical look, and I motioned "later."

Once in the car, I told my husband while Tony was showing him all the guy stuff—property lines, septic, pumps, etc. and so forth—Reka and I had a good chat. I told him every piece of the conversation. "I don't think she's going to take no for an answer. She said she wasn't in charge of this real estate deal. God was. How was I supposed to argue with that?"

He shook his head in disbelief. Here was my big bear of a husband totally baffled by the tiny woman—just like I had been.

"Reka even said she had flat out told God after her first husband died, He literally had to show her—without a shadow of a doubt—who she was supposed to sell her time-treasured home to. She told God she wanted someone to love and care for the house, learning valuable life lessons as she had. She shared she prayed whomever God had planned to buy the house might be able to become friends with her daughter, Riki and husband, Doug and their pre-teen kids living next door—showing them through our lives that God wasn't just about going to church—it was about being "real" and a having a personal friendship and relationship with God."

"Talk about a hefty challenge."

I shifted in my seat to look at my husband. "Bill, she said she *knew* we were the ones to have the house. When I asked her how she knew, she said it was after she shared with me about nursing Dick with cancer and the bible verse she clung to what she held onto, and I shared some of our journeys with cancer and about our life verses."

"Well, I guess we better hear them out. But Care…we can't afford that house."

I turned back to the window and lifted my frazzled thoughts to God. How could we tell this passionate lady no and not hurt her feelings?

Arriving at the local Café, we were greeted like long-lost relatives as Tony and Reka introduced us, table by table, to the patrons of the Café. Grabbing their personalized coffee mugs from what the locals called the "family wall," Reka told us *our* personalized coffee mugs will be hanging there before long, too.

Forty-five minutes later, after a full country biscuit and gravy breakfast, Reka pulled out a legal pad and wrote out a contract.

We looked at each other and shared a glance. The least we could do was to look it over. So we did. My heart was in my shoes.

Reka and Tony insisted on holding the contract. The document Reka drew up stated the set amount we were to pay them each month for rent. Once our house had sold, the contract was to be amended to reflect our entire rental payments were to be applied toward the final purchase price. At the end of the document, we saw the final purchase price. Bill and I looked at each other, in total shock. We hadn't said a word about what our budgeted price was. The price they wrote on the contract was *exactly, to the dollar*, what we had budgeted. It was *my* turn for tears to roll down my rosy cheeks.

We signed the paperwork and even got it notarized—right there at the diner—maple syrup smudges and all.

Tony piped up, "Of *course* someone at the diner is a notary public—you're home!!"

"See?" Reka added, with a delightful smile upon her face. "I told you God keeps His promises and answered my prayer to find just the right people! He must know you two aren't just *any* body!"

"There you go… the house is yours. Welcome to the family!"

And with that, they paid for our meals and gave us a quick hug. We watched as they hopped on Tony's motorcycle and zoomed down the highway.

Bill and I stared at each other…

What in the world just happened?

Bill finally spoke. "God, Reka and Tony just happened, that's what."

41

MOVING MIRACLES

We returned from our weekend away to be greeted by the barrage of questions as if we were contestants on one of Aunt Betty's favorite TV game shows, *Jeopardy*. We could tell if the answer we gave was in the plus or minus column by the looks reflected on Aunt Betty and the kids' faces.

For the most part, our answers landed in the plus column. Categories ranged from new property, number of rooms, activities available, and weather. The final question had the category name of *Recreation Spots*. Happily, we came up with the correct answer: "What is: We don't have to get rid of the boat or snowmobiles?"

Monday morning, we began the process of putting the house up for sale and collecting boxes to start packing our things. Bill was worried no one wanted to buy a house still in a state of remodeling. I walked over to him, wrapped my arms around him, and pestered him saying, "What…you think there isn't another man like you who *loves* to buy and move into a DIY-fixer upper?" (I coyly added I was already praying for the wife—who was probably hoping for a ready-to-move-in/ turn-key house!)

Once again, we witnessed God is a detail man, and walks before us just as a father walks ahead of his children down an unknown path, or a shepherd walking before his flock as they travel great distances to a new pasture. Two short days after putting a "House for Sale" ad in the local newspaper, Bill picked up and answered the ringing telephone. It was a couple who wanted to come and see the house…in ten minutes.

He said, "Sure! C'mon over! Be warned–what you see is what you get—we're in the middle of a mess!" He hung up the phone and informed me some people were coming to see the house, and would be here in about ten minutes.

"They will be here in ten minutes?!" I shrieked. "There is no way we can be ready to show this place off in ten minutes! Are you *crazy?*"

"I'm not crazy, Lady. Remember this is *God's* gig and not ours. He's got this."

I sighed. *Will I ever learn that God is in control, so I don't need or have to be?* I looked around the house as the same thought ran over and over again.

Just then, a car drove into our driveway. It was time for me to put my "walking your talk" adage into action.

We showed the people the house, the shop and garage, the backyard complete with the family-size above ground swimming pool. Next, we toured Aunt Betty's bungalow. We apologized for being in the middle of the mess of packing *and* Bill trying to finish up the remodel.

They were totally unfazed by it all.

The men went back to the garage to talk, while the wife and I walked around the yard, admiring the various flowers and bushes in bloom.

The men soon joined us, and we chit-chatted for several more minutes. The man then looked at Bill and asked him if they could make an offer on the spot, adding if we accepted the offer, we needed to be out in two weeks plus leave *all* the remodeling materials behind as part of the sale.

Bill shot a glance at me and I said to him, "You're the boss around here, you do what you think is best."

As the men walked away, I kept repeating to myself, "*God has this all under control. I don't have to stick my two cents worth in. Bill will do the right thing.*"

The men went aside, presumably to discuss the deal and bounce numbers back and forth. His wife and I walked out of hearing range, so we had no clue what dickering was taking place.

The men walked back over to us.

"Well Lady... looks like we will not be renting after all!" he beamed. "We'll be out of here in ten days!" A huge grin broke out on his face as he shared the news. The other couple also sported big grins, their conversation bubbling over with excitement about "how perfect this place is." The couple shared a personal detail with us.

The wife shared, "We have been on our knees in prayer, asking God to lead us straight to the place He had prepared for us. We needed something *fast* and I tried *so* hard to believe God could really find us what we needed... and wanted. And He did—right down to the details of a separate mother-in-law house for my aged mother and a pool for the grandkids."

Her words made me blush and cringe in shame. I hadn't fully trusted Bill *or* God regarding the sale of the house. I didn't believe that *all* things *could* work out: in the exact way and in the exact time God saw fit. No one needed to say to me, "I told you so."

We set a date to meet at the bank to do the paperwork and said our good-byes. As they drove off, Bill shook his head, "Pinch me. Did this just happen? I mean, God not only brought someone to buy the house, He brought an answer to all our prayers about this place." He humbly continued, "I saved the best news for last. They *insisted* on buying it for *over* the asking price. It will be enough for us to pay for the move and more...*who does that?*"

It was a rhetorical question that need not be answered. Bill and I both *knew* Who does that!

This was one more example our "normal" certainly didn't fit the dictionary's definition of normal. We were beginning to realize part of our calling was to be ready at all times, as sometimes the warning is short. We were to be mobile at-the-end-of-our-hand missionaries. We were to be ready, right where we were at, on any given day.

Murphy's Law and *Ripley's Believe It or Not* couldn't hold a candle to our adventures.

42

FOREVER FRIENDS

Two short weeks after showing the house, we made the migration to the eastern part of the state. We chose to leave after dinnertime. That way we could get over the Cascade Mountain Range while it was still daylight, when traffic was lighter and more manageable. Bill drove a medium-sized moving truck with an attached car trailer. We had finally sold Old Blue, so I drove the "new-to-us" pick-up truck with an extended long-bed cab. With a big load, we were not in a hurry. We took our time and many rest stops at historical markers, truck stops, even just the side of the wide open road to stretch legs and get snacks out for our hollow-legged teens.

The night sky began to sparkle with stars we rarely saw, due to city lights. The kids, Aunt Betty and I looked out our windows, mesmerized by the Milky Way. Suddenly, Tim's voice interrupted my thoughts, "What is *that* in the sky, Mom?"

Looking out both the front and side windows, I wondered as much as Tim did. The night sky turned various hues of green, yellow, and light reds pulsed and washed across the flat desert skies in waves.

"Are they UFOs? The kids asked.

"They are marvelous, whatever they are. I've never seen anything like it in my life." Aunt Betty declared.

I signaled Bill, who was driving behind me, to pull over so we might ask him if he knew what we were looking at. Bill informed us they were the Northern Lights. He had heard on the radio this was one of the very rare times they could be seen this far south, due to a solar flare. The Aurora Borealis, their scientific name, are typically seen only in Alaska and Canada. Since traffic was sparse, we watched the Aurora's shape-shift, change colors, and pulse across the farmland skies under which we were parked.

After a half hour of watching the Aurora's dance overhead, the wagon-train master—Bill—said, "Wagons Ho! Head 'em up, move 'em out!" prompting us to get back into the vehicles and keep driving to our new home. The kids continued to watch the heavenly wonders out their car windows with amazement until slumber over-took their heavy-laden eyes. The light show followed us all the way to our destination.

In the wee hours of a new day, after more than six hours of driving, stopping, and driving some more, my travel weary eyes and muscle-aching body made itself known. Groaning as I got out of my vehicle when we stopped to get gas, I looked at my husband. It was apparent, he was feeling it too. We decided it might be wise to stop and stay the rest of the night at a motel.

Conveniently, there was a reputable chain motel located right next to the truck-stop. We could get a couple decent hours of sleep plus have a good continental-style breakfast before we made the last forty-five minute jaunt to our new home. It was a decision we were glad we made. We knew tired teen tirades, hunger or hormonal driven drama could easily sabotage what we hoped to accomplish later in the day. Thankfully, sleep and an all-they-could-eat breakfast staved off those typical teen 'tudes.

We called Reka to apprise her of our travel plans and itinerary. She asked us to toot the truck horn as we passed their house, which was located on the two-lane highway leading into the small town proper.

Unbeknownst to us, she and several others had organized a day of blessing us beyond measure. The truck horn "toot" was Reka's signal to start the "Family-Phone-Tree" alerting members of the community to head out to our pink brick home—ready to greet us, help unload the moving trailer and truck, plus bring a potluck with enough food to feed an army. Each family also brought items for old-fashioned food-pounding, bringing items to fill our pantry and freezer, so we could focus on getting everyone settled in to our new home and jobs.

What a wonderful way to be welcomed into a community. The trailer and truck were unloaded in no time at all, which left the afternoon to sit in the warmth of the sun and new friends—not to mention sample the many homemade culinary delights. The troop had this spread down to a science. Each family had brought lawn chairs to sit on. Sawhorses topped with plywood and then covered with colorful tablecloths, allowed the impromptu feast to be set up under the shade of a large apple tree. Insulated containers filled with ice kept beverages cold. Kids of all ages played in the creek, and cycled through impromptu volleyball or basketball games, their laughter filling the air.

Yep…Tony, Reka and so much more had happened to us in the area we called home for the next eight years. Because of the warm welcome, the kids made new friends quickly, which made their transition into middle and high school much easier. It felt good to be in the country again, with our closest neighbor, Doug and Riki, and their two kids (who were close in age to our kids) were only several acres away.

We became, and still are, close friends with Doug and Riki. Through thick and thin, raising kids, and both men working construction, it was nice to have someone to walk life with. Our neighbors were two incredible people God placed in our lives and we in theirs, where the bonds of friendship and the grace and love of God grew. Doug and Riki's friendship is an Eternal treasure to be sure. Only God (and Reka!) knew how much we needed the friendship—back then and forever.

Some friends come for a season and then they are gone. Some friendships are near, some friends a continent away. Sometimes it may be years before you reconnect. Some friendships are designed for a specific reason. Maybe to help us adjust our armor, or our attitude, or just to encourage us in the daily battle we call life.

The blessing is, friends are friends forever—especially when God is smack dab in the middle of it.

43

THE GIRLS

Aunt Betty enjoyed the new adventure of moving … at least for the first several months. The weather in the summer and fall were similar to her former home in California, where she lived before moving in with us.

When winter skies and colder temperatures settled in, we began to notice a subtle change in Aunt Betty. We couldn't quite put our finger on *what* was changing, but something definitely was. She began to spend more time in her spacious bedroom. At night, I occasionally heard her soft cries. When I asked her if something was wrong, she denied any scenario I brought up.

One day, I unintentionally overheard her phone conversation with one of The Girls. She sniffled as she related she missed them terribly but didn't want to tell us because we had done so much for her. She told her closest friend, Edith, she wanted to move back to be with them.

After Aunt Betty got off the phone, I asked her to join me in our afternoon tea cup of tea and girl-time before the kids or Bill got home. We chatted about ordinary things like we always did. But then I took a deep breath and told her I'd overheard part of her conversation with Edith. I asked her to be honest with me about how she felt.

She started to cry and whimpered out the words, "Yes, I miss The Girls terribly, but you've been so good to me, I didn't want to say anything."

I told her that her happiness was what was important to us. I apologized for not being sensitive to *her* needs or realizing living in the country was a total life-style alteration for her. We discussed what options she had and what steps she needed to take for her to move back to be by "The Girls". The biggest hurdle was the apartment she formerly lived in wasn't available, but she could be put on a waiting list.

We knew it could take months for an apartment to become vacant. Aunt Betty understood the circumstances and was willing to wait.

After the decision had been made, Aunt Betty's countenance improved immensely. Every couple of weeks I called the complex manager to check on her wait list status. The manager confided in me she had really missed Aunt Betty. She had been one of her all-time favorite tenants.

Six weeks after Aunt Betty put her name on the apartment waiting list, she received a call an apartment would be available in two weeks. Asked if she still wanted to move, Aunt Betty's answer was am emphatic and affirming, "Yes!"

As we moved Aunt Betty back to her new apartment, the manager told me with a mischievous little grin, she had put Aunt Betty's name at the top of the list, since she had been a former (and favorite) tenant. So much for rules!

The Girls were reunited. Aunt Betty's new apartment was close to the manager's office as well as the laundry room—which gave *me* a measure of confidence in her safety. Her unit was also two units closer to Edith and Gladys, two of her closest friends. It was another God-wink for me, assuring me my great-aunt was going to be looked after. I wasn't anticipating the deep heartache and sadness I experienced as I drove away. I felt like I was abandoning her. She had lived with us, literally or near-by, for twelve years.

Eating Oreos™ has never been the same.

Aunt Betty flourished back in her familiar routine of being with The Girls. They attended garden club meetings, senior center activities, and were involved with church friends and Senior Sunday School class.

The family who Bill had rock-drilled for took her under their wings. They invited Aunt Betty to their house for blueberry pancakes before church, took her out for meals and made sure she kept up with her medical appointments. Their kids became *her* kiddos and she felt a special part of their family, and they hers. Once again, our friends were "Jesus with skin on."

Every couple of months I drove the five hours to spend time with Aunt Betty. Occasionally she came back with me for a week-long visit. Anything more than a week was beginning to be too much for her. She was approaching her mid-nineties, and noticeably starting to slow down. As time marched on, slowly, one by one, The Girls went Home to be with the Lord whom they so loved. It was hard to watch from a distance. It was agonizing for Aunt Betty.

Up until 1998, our family and our close friends, along with another couple in Centralia, had been the primary care-watchers for Aunt Betty. Over the years, due to various factors and life circumstances, my siblings had intermittent interaction with Aunt Betty. Next to me, family-wise, Aunt Betty was closest to my oldest sister, who lived two hours away. She occasionally made the drive to see Aunt Betty and take her to visit at her home from time to time, graciously loving on her and keeping a family eye on her.

Aunt Betty's health began to deteriorate to the point she could no longer safely live on her own. I knew the eastern part of the state was not a place she wanted to be. With a heavy heart, I turned to my oldest sister. After several falls, a broken hip, and congestive heart failure, Aunt Betty was moved into a graduated care facility near my sister's home. It was not an easy decision for my sister and me, or for the friends who had loved and watched over her.

As often is the case in geriatric care, once a decline starts, the soul and will to live closely follow. Aunt Betty's health and well-being declined rapidly. Lying in bed one night, an over-whelming nudge came over me. I knew I needed to get over to see her… right then and there. I told Bill and he insisted I go see Aunt Betty. He assured me he and the kids could handle things. Hastily, I threw a couple changes of clothes in a backpack, grabbed some granola bars and caffeinated sodas to keep me awake, and took off.

I was glad I made the middle of the night trip. I arrived in time to spend what turned out to be one of her last days. As we held hands, she looked at me and said "You know I never wanted to live to be seventy, or eighty, much less over ninety. Thank you for filling my last years with faith, family, friends, and fun, and leading me to a personal and special friendship with God. Go now and take the Oreos™ home to the kiddos and Bill, will you?"

She closed her eyes and lapsed into a coma. I knew she was on her way Home…at peace and more than ready to be reunited with her Johnny, The Girls, and the Lord she had come to know and love in a very personal way. She was ninety-four-years-young.

What a way The Girls had shown us. Not only how to *live* life, but how to *finish well*.

44

HAMMERING AWAY

True to their promise, the union kept Bill as busy as he wanted to be. He oversaw several jobs including: building an addition onto the regional headquarters of a chain bakery, building a new fast-food restaurant, being one of the superintendents on a hydroelectric dam job, and a foreman for the new construction of a waste water treatment facility.

Two years of union jobs and my working as a rural school OT during the school year and home health in the summers, allowed us to save and put money aside to build my dream house. We had loved living in the pink brick house and establishing ourselves in the community. We were glad we had told Reka when we bought the house our goal was to hopefully build our own place someday, so buying the pink brick house wasn't a forever purchase.

So, there was no surprise when the day came to start circulating the word around the community we were looking for a piece of property to buy, so Bill could build me my dream house. A house that was *not* a remodel, or a fixer-upper, but new and *completely* finished before we moved into it house.

I didn't hold my breath, often quoting the phrase, "A cobbler's kids never have shoes, just like a carpenter's wife never has a home completely finished!" I often mused, "I wonder if Mary always travelled with Jesus, following him where he went, not to be a helicopter mom but leaving her husband, Joseph (a carpenter) behind to finish *her* house and honey-do list! Guess I'll have to ask her when I meet her in Eternity. We know *that* House is finished!"

Within a month of putting the word out, a family in our church approached us, telling us they were being transferred out of state, and needed to sell their single-wide mobile home on a twenty-acre homestead. They asked if we were interested in buying it. We told them we'd love to look at it and set a time for later in the day.

When we went to look at it, it appeared to be perfect, including a full view of Mount Spokane to "go up to the hills, bearers of Good News." The land was situated on several levels and elevations. The varied terrain was perfect for hiking, snowmobiling, or an evening stroll to think, pray and enjoy the beauty of our surroundings. Bill liked the varied terrain as it left several good building sites for the house and the combination barn, shop, and apartment he was planning to build, as well as an area to put up a henhouse and goat shed.

The property included a one hundred-year-old apple orchard with several varieties of apples, two plum trees, and a colossal lilac bush. A year-round creek ran through the acreage, and several well-worn paths meandered up, down and around the different parts of the property.

We spotted a small shack at the bottom of a hill that couldn't have been more than five hundred square feet. The owners told us the shed was used mainly during hunting season to hang their bounty before processing it.

We ended the tour of the property with the four adults joining hands as we prayed for God's guidance, wisdom, and discernment for what, how, and who *He* wanted to be stewards of this property. This was important as the property had been homesteaded over one hundred years earlier, by people who had claimed the land for God.

Bill told the owners we would make a decision regarding the

property in a few days. As we drove away and bounced down the gravel road, I looked over at Bill. The last rays of the evening sun shone on his face, giving it a golden radiance. He glanced back at me and chuckled, "Well…that's a no-brainer! But let's still pray about it a couple days."

I agreed.

Three days later we set a date to meet with the owners. Bill re-iterated his words and the owners chuckled and said they felt the same way.

It looked like we'd be making another move. Luckily this time, it was only seven miles away, and Bill could get living quarters ready before we put the pink brink house on the market. It took two months to close and sign the legal papers. Within a week of closing, the former owners moved out, and we started our new adventure.

And what an adventure it was. Turning to God wasn't our *only* option during the adventure, but it was the *right* option. We were sure glad God knew *all* about it, way before it happened—curve-balls and all.

45

GREAT EXPECTATIONS

We were not expecting to discover the mobile home that was on the property we bought was not safe to inhabit. But it wasn't.

The floors had been covered with clothes and clutter when we looked at it, so we never saw the true condition of the single-wide trailer. The floorboards were rotted, literally, with gaping holes to the ground below. My *not* favorite creatures of God, mice, had staked their claim in every room, and mold was climbing up every wall. The wiring to the main electric panel was a nightmare. At least I didn't find a wayward mouse in the breaker box! Only by the grace of God and His watchful eye had prevented a fire or accident from occurring while people lived in it. It was no wonder few people were ever invited over to this home for a visit.

Bill and I pondered what to do about this unexpected glitch. We *knew* we couldn't live in the trailer. While financially we were able to make two mortgage payments, we knew the danger of double debt and wanted to avoid and steer clear of financial fiasco, plus we didn't want to dip into the new-house-funds we had set aside.

We decided to put the pink brick house up for sale or rent right away, knowing if by some miracle there was quick action, we could always write in the agreement a negotiable closing date, allowing Bill time to come up with a plan of where *we* might lay our heads at night.

Leave it to my DIY'er and farm-boy husband to come up with the idea of fixing the little shack at the bottom of the hill into temporary living quarters. He thought he could get it fixed up in a couple weeks – at least into being in livable condition. The kids were excited. Me? Not so much. I wished I had some of their exuberance with the ability to always be ready and anticipating adventure.

Even though I was hesitant, I gave Bill my nod of approval. I put one condition on my approval: after he fixed up the shack for our *temporary* dwelling, he had to promise to build the shop/barn with upstairs studio apartment *first*. It was time for my carpenter to have a nice place to hang his tools and keep his equipment—plus we could use the room for storage.

It was settled. The timing couldn't have been more perfect for Bill. Since he was in between his next union job starting up, and it was late spring, he had many sunny, warm days to build and create to his heart's content.

We moved into our temporary quarters within a month, bringing with us only the bare necessities. The rest we placed in a storage unit until we could properly move into the new house. Once it was built, of course.

True to Reka's original prayer with us, God brought another not-just-*any*body in need of the blessings of living in the pink brick house—all in His impeccable timing and not a day sooner than needed. As we moved out one weekend, the following weekend the new owners moved in.

Back at the new property, Bill worked quickly to get the shed ready for us to move into. He built two sleeping lofts, one on either end of the A-frame cabin—formerly called shed—for the kids. They could each fit a twin mattress and a small dresser on their loft floor, and had a portable ladder to pull up or down to get to their room or our living space. I slept on our recliner and

Bill slept on the couch. We all slept in sleeping bags to keep bedding laundry at a minimum. We felt like the family portrayed on the television show, *The Walton's*. When we each settled into our sleeping spots at night, someone usually piped up saying, "Good night, John Boy…Good night, Jim Bob…" Oh! The stories those 500 square-foot-cabin walls could tell!

The electricity load was fragile. One breaker or another was forever going off. It was easy to forget not to use the toaster while mom was making her morning coffee. Or, the curling iron couldn't be used at the same time as the microwave. Our front porch door was our only house door. It opened into the modified bathroom where the hot water tank, a small toilet, and very small shower were all in one tiny space. We came up with a signal and posted a sign outside that said:

DO NOT ENTER IF OUTSIDE LIGHT IS ON!

The sign meant someone was using the bathroom. Unbelievably there were only two or three times when someone forgot to look for the light signal—of course it was *me*!

Looking back, I can't believe we lived in the shed turned cabin. It was our daughter's senior year in high school. I was not only working, but I was in my final month of extension classes for my Master's Degree in Education. It was going to allow me to bump up on the pay scale and the retirement tier as an occupational therapist, plus giving me credentials to be a guest lecturer or substitute teacher/professor.

Two weeks after receiving my Master's Degree diploma, I was working at a school three-hour drive from our home. Something in my upper thigh didn't *feel* right. I kept working for an hour or two, until I got one of those still-small-voice intuitions. I went to the principal telling him I had an emergency medical issue and needed to leave immediately. Concerned, knowing I had a three-hour drive, he asked me to check in with him every thirty minutes.

The still small voice was right. It was another DES-related cancer rearing its ugly head. This time it was a lymphoma. What I had felt was an aggressive tumor in my groin. It had a prolific blood supply, making it grow swiftly. In less than four hours, it had grown from the size of a small pea to the size of a quarter.

Blessedly, I caught it early, and surgery was the only treatment regime required. One more battle, one more obstacle. Recuperating from surgery in the tiny cabin was certainly an adventure. I can't say it was a simple process, but by keeping our tenets of faith, family, and fun, we grew closer together as a family. And living and recuperating in five-hundred-square-feet was *close*!

By Thanksgiving time, Bill had his two-story shop and barn framed and roofed. The top floor was a studio apartment. He planned it that way so as soon as the building was closed in, we could move our combination stove and oven, our full-size refrigerator, washer and dryer out of storage. No more hot plate or trips to the laundry mat. Yay! The apartment also had a hide-a-bed couch that could be used as an alternate bedroom for the kids.

The hill to and from the A-frame cabin and shop was steep. Oftentimes it was too muddy or icy to use our regular vehicles to get back and forth. Instead we shuttled using our snowmobiles or four-wheelers to commute to our vehicles, transport hot meals or freshly folded laundry.

In the one year we lived in the A-frame, I think the only casualty we incurred was losing the freshly baked Thanksgiving rolls as we zipped up and down the hill on the snow machines and hit a bump a little too fast. Modern day pioneers!

46

COMPUTERS AND CHICKEN FEET

By far, one of the best Family Night inspired memories we have was planning and going on a family foreign missions trip to Tobago, West Indies. Bill had been on a men's trip to Tobago, to help finish building a church. Prior to Bill's departure back to the United States, the church members asked him, "Brudder (Brother) Bill will you bring your family to visit your Second Home? We want to meet them!"

We brought the invitation up during one of our Family Nights. We shared with Jamie and Tim we had been praying for years that we could take them on a mission trip before they flew the coop. But, travelling to the Caribbean had not been on our radar as a destination—tickets were pricey, especially for a family of four.

Once more, our prayers were answered in ways above and beyond what we could ever ask, think or imagine. A distant relative had recently passed away. In their will they had bequeathed our family with a financial gift—a gift that was one hundred dollars over the amount of what four round-trip tickets would cost. It was an affirmation about trusting God, a tangible lesson in God's provision. It was also a reminder our prayers are always heard, and answered in due time—His time. We would be going on the foreign mission field as a family, at last.

Our kids thought the best time to go to Tobago would be their upcoming Spring Break. It coincided with the Tobagonian and surrounding Caribbean Island's combined traditional festivities and celebrations commemorating Easter Week.

Tobago was where the original Walt Disney™ movie *Swiss Family Robinson*™ was filmed. The house where we stayed was only blocks from the tree that originally held the infamous tree house.

Tim—our son—was a computer whiz for his high school. The Tobagonians gave him the opportunity to help set up and give instruction on how to use the small island's *very first* school computer. He was in I.T. Heaven!

Jamie served at a Soup Kitchen at a homeless shelter, where she was introduced to the cuisine of homemade chicken soup—Tobagonian style. That meant the soup was served with the *full* chicken foot –claws and all, sticking out of the bowl. She did her very best to not show her disdain (or faint!) and to her credit, even tried *one* bite of a claw. Her brother came to her rescue – he *loved* the claws, devouring them quickly—much to the Tobagonians' delight!

Bill was kept busy doing various, much needed carpentry work. I volunteered with the local women—also learning a new cuisine and assisting them with cooking meals for the five days of Holy Week: Maundy Thursday through Easter Monday. They adhered to their custom that no cooking should take place during what many of them believed is the holiest time of year.

Christian Tobagonians believed all attention should be focused on their religious traditions of Easter. All island businesses shut down, including stores, and most corner kiosks. The only kiosks open were ones selling water or juices, since it was so warm, and hydration was imperative. Experiencing and celebrating Easter with them was amazing. And there wasn't a shred of evidence of an Easter basket, Easter eggs, or candy.

Most of the people on the island did not drive—they walked.

They walked to the kiosks or stores, to their jobs, and to church. And during this special Easter time, they walked a mile or so to their churches each of the five days.

The Holy Week services started at 8:00 a.m. Those who were part of the prayer team arrived at 7:00 and prayed over every pew, chair, and corner of the church. The service had no time constraints, and often lasted for three to four hours.

People were dressed in their finest attire. All ages sat in the sanctuary for the full service. The church had no glass window panes – just open spaces where windows would be. The worship was beautiful. Simple instruments and voices were raised to the heavens. Prayer time lasted a good hour after the sermon. After the morning service people would walk home for "a rest." Another Easter week service was held later in the afternoon.

In the following four evenings, we attended a most amazing event. People trekked several miles to the city-square amphitheater where people from the island and surrounding Caribbean islands gathered for an Easter worship celebration extravaganza. It began at 7:00 p.m. and lasted until the wee hours of the morning. The music each evening was unbelievable. The voices were phenomenal.

Now, let me paint the picture for you: We were the *only* light-skinned people in a sea of Caribbean, dark-skinned people. Bill's large, physical frame, with vocal pipes to match, made heads turn when he sang along, worshipping with the audience. We kinda stood out in the crowd.

During an intermission, a chorus of people started chanting, "Brudder Bill! Sing Brudder Bill! Sing Mrs. Brudder Bill!"

While it wasn't part of the plan, and we both felt awkward, we relented.

We sang a beloved song by Michael W. Smith.

"And friends are friends forever, if the Lord's the Lord of

them…" Our voices rose as the depth of the words pierced our hearts. These people… this place… had become beloved to us all.

Tears streamed down faces in the audience as thunderous applause shook the stage, accompanied by a standing ovation. A spontaneous chorus of praise to God broke out. Little did we know that we were being recorded by their one local, rudimentary television station.

Sadly and unbeknownst at the time, it was the last time Bill and I sang publicly together.

47

DREAMS DO COME TRUE

The day finally arrived when Bill turned my dream house plans into the County Building Permit Office. Bill told the permit officer we had recently read a newspaper article about the County's newly formed task force to address the growing needs and issues concerning disability-friendly and accessible housing.

He told the official he had specifically designed the plans for our house to be disability-friendly for me—and he was offering our accessible design plans as a prototype for the task force to consider. We felt it was one way we could give back to the community. Bill suggested to the County officials that the task force members could watch, take notes, ask questions, or give feedback throughout the building process.

The officials gratefully accepted his offer. It was a bonus for them and a pleasure for us. Bill was known by area contractors and union officials for his excellent work in the building trade. They also knew me as a local school and home health occupational therapist, who lived with multiple health issues and orthopedic hidden disabilities, plus I had credentials in ergonomic and adaptive design and had consulted on other building projects over my career.

My dream house was a 1700 square-foot, Ranch-style home, with a 2300 square-foot cedar deck that could be accessed from four places throughout the house. The concrete walkway up to the house was lined with above-ground cedar boxes filled with pansies (my favorite) and red geraniums.

The extra-wide entryway was made to accommodate wheelchairs. There was an office off to one side, and a combined laundry room/pantry on the other. The entry then opened into one large, spacious area with a spectacular geometric-designed, vaulted pine ceiling. The open-concept area showcased the accessible living, dining, and kitchen areas. Floor to ceiling picture windows and a door to the outside deck, allowed one to view the property's orchard, creek, and valley to Mt. Spokane.

The kitchen had a multi-level island—perfect for families with small children, people who used wheelchairs, and especially for me with my varied medical issues. Three additional countertops were also at varied heights. The refrigerator was raised for my specific height and accessibility needs with my fused and bolted back and bionic shoulders. The front-load washer and dryer were on pedestals, eliminating my need to bend over and made it possible for laundry to be at my lap level —which was especially nice after one of my surgical procedures or rehabilitation seasons.

A broad hallway off the living area led to three bedrooms and two bathrooms, all with extra wide doorways. One of the bathrooms had a shower with a seat built into it and included an optional hand-held shower unit installed, if needed. The second bathroom had a tub/shower combination, with a transfer slide and shower chair available. The cabinets and shelves in both bathrooms were built to be accessible by someone who may use a wheelchair. While the design was for me, it was a practical and visual demonstration for the building officials, illustrating what an accessible home could look like.

A favorite feature of the house was the hot tub. You could access it through the master bedroom door or side living area door. The hot tub itself was recessed into the deck, had handicap accessible railings and steps. We also had a Hoyer lift if needed, to lift people in and out of the hot tub. The hot tub was one of the most used amenities of the house!

Once summer rolled around again, we added an above ground pool for the kids (and us!) to enjoy during their final year(s) of living at home. We also added a terraced family garden…or should I say "deer" garden, as they usually partook of the fruits of our labor before we did.

During the seven years we lived on the property, we often saw and hear the resident wild turkey flock. Deer grazed on the grassland and peacefully rested and bedded down at the creek's edge. We watched rotund bear cubs as they learned to climb. We especially enjoyed watching the little rascals try to climb up the heavy-laden apple trees. The cubs inched their way up a tree until they found a sturdy branch to sit on. They enjoyed the hard-earned fruits of their labor as they plucked and munched away on the yet un-picked apples, eating to their heart's content. After they had filled their round little bellies, they laid back and took naps. It made us laugh when they fell out of the tree—quite a rude awakening.

It truly was my *dream* house. As Bill built it, he painted in *huge* letters on the newly, plywood covered roof:

I LOVE YOU!

The phrase was big enough to be seen (and video-taped) by a local television helicopter that happened to fly over. It was televised on the evening newscast. The endearment is permanently etched in my mind and on my heart. Someday, when a future owner re-roofs the house, will *they* have a surprise!

The kids lived their final teen-aged years in the various habitats of our dream property as they were built. We let each of our kids live in the upstairs of the barn in the studio apartment during the latter half of their senior year of high school. It allowed them to learn and get used to living on their own, yet still have us close by. The kids could decorate as they wanted and arrange furniture the way that suited them. They were expected to do their own laundry, dishes, and general up-keep of the apartment, but they were *always* welcome to come down the hill for meals or come back home to their old bedroom whenever they wanted.

We acted as their landlords. Rent was bartered for by helping with extra chores, or in lieu of their allowance. We respected their privacy, promising not to barge in on them without notice. Being true landlords, we *did* schedule occasional inspections of the apartment. They knew if a pink tag was found on the door the "Mother-Board-of-Health" (me) had condemned it. They knew being pink-tagged meant "please clean your apartment or face eviction back to the main house!" In retrospect it was one of the wiser parental decisions we made. They learned life-skills, responsibility, and were given a bit of freedom from parents. I hoped transitioning to an empty nest gradually might be easier on this mama's heart when they did move out for good, totally on their own.

Our four family tenets were well entrenched as we lived out our last seven years together. Soon, it was time for the kids to leave the nest. The years had flown by quickly. We had watched the kids learn to deal with success as well as failure. We *all* grew through the roller coaster of hormones, friends, learning to drive (and crash), and dating. The kids, once again, had been *more* than Super Troopers.

With God's help we did our best to raise them up and give them deep roots. It was now time to let them try their wings and fly.

Some days were easier said than done. Just sayin'.

48

SO WHAT DOES DISABILITY LOOK LIKE?

Recently, I was listening to one of Joni Eareckson Tada's radio clips. She was talking about Family Retreats. As I listened, I reminisced about the day I went to check in at Family Retreat.

The registrar looked at me and asked, "You *do* know this is for families with a disability, don't you?"

I replied, "Yes, I do. My son has mild cerebral palsy and autistic tendencies from abuse and neglect before we adopted him and my daughter—also adopted—has a genetic heart disorder. And, I have a disability as well."

She looked at me and exclaimed, "Well! You three don't *look* disabled!"

I bit my tongue so hard I thought it might bleed. Instead, I smiled and thanked her for helping us get registered.

The OT and the mom in me, who dealt 24/7 with disability, pondered the question. "*So… what does disability look like?*"

Looking back, I recognized it was and *is* a great question to ask. Not only twenty-five-plus years ago, but today as well.

It's amazing to see how far disability awareness has come—and how much further there is to go.

Think back to the different names you've heard over the years describing someone with a disability. The politically correct word changes as often as the wind. Is a person handicapped? Are they slow? Maybe they are Developmentally Delayed? Severely injured? Intellectually disabled? Blind? Visually impaired? Deaf? Hearing impaired? One has to stay on their toes to keep up with the correct vernacular or politically correct words to use.

But what does disability *look* like?

It was not unusual to have people tell me I didn't look (or act) disabled. For my entire life, I have lived with hidden disabilities— whether it is my non-existent immune system from exposure to DES, multiple orthopedic and neurological impairments, my brain injury, or cancer. My "normal" changes each and every day I wake up.

It still does. I'm sure it is the same for others. We can't always see when a person has autism/autistic tendencies, or other spectrums of mental or physical health conditions. We often miss seeing the hidden stress issues related to a job or finances… or the amazing load of stress from dealing with the myriad of medical mazes and mounting medical costs.

When our son was younger, his autistic tendencies (he is high on the spectrum) earned him various, sometimes unkind nicknames. Bouts with mental health issues, speech delays, and the nuances of autism could wear our entire family's patience thin. There were days when I was so frustrated with his autistic nuances that before thinking I blurted out, "How can you be *so* bright, but act so *stupid*?"

Great mom moments. I know.

It was years before he shared how hard it had been for him. The depression and difficulty making friends were challenging – especially in his teen years. Taking Advanced Placement and Gifted classes yet be labelled *Special Ed* because of the OT, PT, and Speech services he needed, was the worst, he shared. Even so, he didn't *look* disabled.

Our daughter didn't look disabled either. We carefully had to monitor how often she ate and what. It wasn't until she was in her thirties it was discovered she had a congenital heart issue. She needed a heart graft and later a full, heart valve replacement.

I was—and will forever be—grateful to Joni and Ken Tada and all who are involved with *Joni and Friends*™ who don't judge a person by their appearance or disability. They looked deep into a person's heart and put words into real actions. Joni and Friends™ gave our kids the opportunity to serve and minister yet be served and ministered to. Our kids' involvement with *Family Retreats and WFTW*™ enlarged their world view. The staff and volunteers modeled, mentored, and encouraged our son and daughter to soar high like eagles, and gave them opportunities and adventures forever etched on their hearts and in their lives.

What does disability look like to you?

Check out **www.joniandfriends.org** to see where you and your family can minister and be ministered to. Disabled or not!

49

WHEELCHAIRS ARE NOT FOR WIMPS!

Our participation in the inaugural *Joni and Friends*™ Family Retreat in 1991 led to my being asked to participate and volunteer on a *Joni and Friends - Wheels for the World*™(WFTW™) wheelchair distribution trip in 1995. On the trip I utilized my Occupational Therapy skills and knowledge, assist with wheelchair distributions and fittings, lead disability awareness sessions, as well as interact with disability outreach organizations and churches. The team consisted of leadership and staff from *Joni and Friends*, occupational and physical therapists, mobility technicians, and laypeople. The team included people who had a disability, and those without a disability.

I was given the opportunity to share as an occupational therapist, as a wife and mother who personally lived with multiple disabilities, and as a mom with two children with special needs. Sharing insights on issues family members and/or individuals with a disability face was a passion of mine.

So off I went.

Many people in the Eastern European areas I visited were astonished to see a woman who was disabled. In 1995, persons with a disability were rarely seen in public. Since I sported a long-leg brace at the time, it was pretty obvious I had an orthopedic impairment. People on the street often gawked and stared at me, but when they gained courage to talk to me, it gave me the chance to share how God has used each challenge and obstacle to grow my faith, increase my courage, and yes, experience victory in the daily battles, too.

On one of our last days, after completing our final wheelchair distribution of wheelchairs and crutches, we were returning from a visit to a family who had invited us to their flat to thank us. After partaking in their time-honored tradition of afternoon tea, as we were leaving, the family thoughtfully reminded us of safety hazards and information our local hosts had given us upon our arrival. Namely, pedestrians have no rights, so be aware and cautious when we crossed a street.

It was good advice, especially in light of our local hosts having shared stories of the difficulty of living with little or no medical services available, much less access to medical supplies.

Sure enough, on our way back to our hotel, a car jumped the curb, and ran over my *good*, left foot, leaving black tire tread marks on my white tennis shoe. My years of training and working as an occupational therapist automatically kicked in. The agonizing, sharp pain alerted me to the possibility I might have broken several bones in my foot.

I did a quick orthopedic assessment. I could see and feel the displaced bones. Additionally, I asked a physical therapist and a nurse who were on our team to look at my injured foot. They both agreed with me – the bones were most likely broken. In light of the lack of medical care or facilities available, the three of us were of the same opinion—it would be best for me to wait until we returned to the United States to seek medical treatment. We were scheduled to be home in three days.

Until then, I followed the protocol physicians and therapists typically use for a broken bone in the United States: three days of ICE (Ice, Compression, and Elevation) which allows swelling to go down before a final diagnosis is given.

There was one problem. I could keep compression on my foot by keeping my laced tennis shoe on. I could elevate my foot when sitting, propping my foot up on another chair or upon extra pillows when I went to bed. But ice?

Ice was a rare commodity to be found. But, no worries! I knew God had this. Why? I was the *only* person on the team who had a room with *no* hot water. Only *ice* cold bath water. Since we couldn't find ice, my only option was to soak my foot in the frigid bath water several times a day.

But, wait! The story gets even better. I was scheduled to meet with the head of a wheelchair manufacturing company that designed sport's wheelchairs for elite athletes… want to take a guess when?

The very next day.

I had no prior knowledge the company was also working on a prototype for an ergonomically designed crutch. The demonstration models were bright red in color.

With God's Divine Intervention, a litany of paperwork, and a lot of prayer, I was able to *purchase* a demonstration pair of the proto-type crutches! To this day, I have never seen the design—even in my stacks of OT mobility catalogs. I continue to use the crutches today—after back, knee or foot surgery, rehab time in a boot cast, on high pain days or if I have long distances to walk.

Once home from the European trip, I went to see my orthopedic physician. He ordered x-rays to determine if indeed my foot was broken. It was – in several places. The orthopedic physician praised me for using the ICE protocol. He told me my quick thinking helped me to avoid surgery. Even so, it was a *long* eight weeks in a boot cast!

When I am out in public using my unique crutches, heads turn to gain a second look. Eyebrows get raised, followed by the predictable question: "Where did you get those *cool* crutches?"

The query is my *God*incidence cue to share my story and testimony. It becomes one more opportunity to share my faith in God and His faithfulness to me in life's daily battles, plus the reminder: *Don't Wimp Out!*

While on the trip, I saw first-hand how a person with limited mobility is often prevented from participating in their community simply because they have no way to get from Point A to Point B, unless someone carried them. A wheelchair or crutches removes barriers, opening doors they never thought imaginable. *Wheels for the World* provided the gift of mobility in the form of a custom-fit wheelchair, along with a Bible and the Gospel message in their native language. The impact of seeing people and hearing their stories—with tears streaming down their cheeks—that now, because of a wheelchair can go to school for the first time, or church, or sit and play, or just enjoy being outside was completely overwhelming to me.

On my first *WFTW* trip, we had many meaningful discussions, conversations and tossed ideas around on how to increase the collection of formerly used, but restorable, wheelchairs. While we were chatting about collections, conversations at the *Joni and Friends* headquarters were held on how to increase the number of prisons willing to partner with Joni and Friends develop wheelchair restoration programs. You see, the collected wheelchairs would be restored to a "like new" condition by inmates who wanted to work on this worthy cause. Those conversations and more ultimately led to my increased involvement with *Wheels for the World*. It was a reminder to me our family's *call* to the mission field had not changed—merely the location.

The Wheels on the Chair Go "Round and 'Round

As *WFTW* grew, I was offered a part-time, self-supporting (Missionary) Ministry Associate position. I worked from home, and not at the headquarters in California. I tele-commuted and flew to headquarters as needed. My official working title was *Western Regional Chair Corp Manager.* My territory covered the states west of the Rocky Mountains.

As one of the regional managers for *WFTW,* I helped the staff develop policies and procedures plus train regional volunteers who collected wheelchairs to be restored. These volunteers—called Chair Corps Representatives—came from churches, civic organizations, medical and allied health professions, schools, and communities. I trained volunteers in my region about collection strategies, help them plan wheelchair collection drives, and teach them how and where to store the wheelchairs once collected.

Keep On Trucking

I was also tasked with developing and implementing a national transportation system for the wheelchairs collected around the country. I communicated with trucking companies, their drivers, airlines, freight companies, and any transportation entity I could think of to help build a transportation network. All this, so we could get the donated chairs from collection sites to storage and processing sites, and eventually to the prisons where inmates restored them. With over 10,000 chairs collected each year, *Wheels for the World* was a growing ministry. Transportation needs were an on-going need. And the need continues to this day. (Hint, hint!)

Second Chances

While I was working on a transportation network, *WFTW* personnel were continuing their work on increasing the numbers of prisons developing and implementing the Prison Wheelchair Restoration Program. In 1995, *Joni and Friends* worked with two prisons. To date, there are now more than twenty prisons involved with *Joni and Friends – Wheels for the World*. Working in the *WFTW* Wheelchair Restoration Shop is so popular, that at many prisons inmates are put on a waiting list—even though it is one of the lowest paying jobs.

Bill and I were given permission to take a truckload of collected chairs directly to one of the prison sites. We observed the inmates at work, meticulously restoring each chair. They told us how they each had an individual logo they would add to each restored chair, so they could "go" wherever the chair went, even though they were incarcerated behind bars.

Several men shared with us how special and important this opportunity was for them. One inmate told us it was the first time in his life he had chance to give back—he had always taken from others. He said it felt good to do something positive and productive, even redeeming. The pride for the work he performed was evident in his voice as he shared, "I'm so glad I get to do this for the rest of my life."

Isn't it amazing how God was using a man sentenced to life in prison without parole? God is the God of second-chances and His unconditional love for each one of us—no matter what we've done—is overwhelming.

The quality of work done to restore wheelchairs was remarkable—the chairs truly looked like new. As we said our good-byes, the inmate we were able to chat with shook our hand and said, "I'll see you in Heaven!"

Because of *Joni and Friends* and *WFTW*, inmates were able to hear the Gospel message. The warden let the inmates listen to Joni's daily radio message. Many inmates' hearts and lives have been changed forever, receiving the grace only God can give… all because of the gift of a wheelchair.

Hands Across the Sea

In 1999, I was asked to represent *Joni and Friends-WFTW*, as they partnered with a British ministry and an Albanian ministry. I would be using the same skills I used when I went on my first outreach. I was the only American woman on the team journeying to this Eastern European country, joined by the Director of Media for *Joni and Friends* and the COO of *Joni and Friends.*

The three of us participated in several wheelchair distributions. On one of our evenings, the team ventured out to a local restaurant. While many enjoyed the local cuisine, we all stayed to drinking *bottled* Coca-Cola®, for health safety reasons. After our supper, as we walked home, we were witness to an automatic-weapon firefight at the highway intersection just a short block away from where we had been minutes before. To say we were grateful for the garrisons and legions of angels God sent to be a hedge of protection around us, was an understatement.

During the last wheelchair distribution on this trip, I had the humbling honor and experience to represent Joni, *Joni and Friends* and *WFTW* in a television interview for an American news outlet.

While waiting for the television videographer to finish setting up his equipment, I started performing some natural OT stretching and range of motion movements on a recipient of a wheelchair. She was born with cerebral palsy and was non-verbal. The wheelchair technicians put the final touches on the wheelchair while I worked to stretch her severely contracted arms from the decades of dealing with the effects of cerebral palsy. Her mother and brother explained to me—through an interpreter—the woman had not been out of her parents' home in over thirty years.

I started humming a chorus as we were waiting. Suddenly, the woman started to make some guttural sounds and began to hum with me, *matching my tune*! Her mother gasped, bringing her hands up over her mouth in utter surprise and shock. Tears began to stream down the Muslim mother's cheeks. The brother could only stand with mouth wide open in disbelief. They had never heard her utter *anything* in her *entire* life.

I didn't realize the reporter was filming what was happening until he asked me, "Why did you even *consider* coming here? Who are *we to you*? And, how can you communicate with this family? You have such different religious beliefs and you don't speak the same language?"

I answered, "Love knows no barriers. Besides being an occupational therapist, I am a mother of a child with special needs. Love is love in any language. Love has no barriers – especially a mother's love, just like God's love."

I cherish the photo I have of the four of us. In it I am kneeling next to the woman as her mother and brother stood behind her in her new wheelchair. This restored, like new wheelchair would allow this woman to go to market for the first time in her life, or other family events. It can't get better than that.

Before they left, I happened to look at the *Joni and Friends-WFTW* tag on her chair. Imagine my heart when I realized the wheelchair just happened to come from one of the chairs my family had collected. Out of the *thousands* of chairs collected, all over the United States, this particular chair had been sent to be restored at the prison Bill and I visited. It had been trucked and delivered to the prison by the very trucker who picked it up at our house *and* it was signed off with the logo of the inmate we had talked to. What are the chances? As Paul Young—author of *The Shack*, son once told him "Only one hundred percent, Dad—because God's in the details!"

I've long believed there are no *co*incidences, only *God*incidences.

50

SEASONS CHANGE AND SO DO LIVES

Once home from the wheelchair distribution overseas, it was physically becoming evident to me; my days and ability to continue as *Western Region Chair Corp Manager* were waning. It was hard for me to admit that my thirty plus years as an OT, my years of bending, lifting, twisting and pushing way past my limits, plus the DES related joint disintegration accelerating in my back and knees were taking their toll.

Joni and Friends™ was gracious to let me transition from *WFTW*™ to *Family Retreats* (FR). As Associate Director, I was able to continue to work from home. I helped develop and implement training manuals for *Short Term Missionaries* (STM's) at Family Retreats held around the country. I was able to attend several of the Family Retreats, in between surgeries, this time as staff, not camper.

In July of 2000, it was time to let my position at *Joni and Friends*™ go. It was one of the hardest things I've ever had to do.

Sitting down in my favorite recliner, a warm cup of coffee in my hands, I watched a pair of eagles soar on thermal winds blowing through the valley. The trees on our property were beginning to turn their majestic fall colors of gold and red, some of the leaves shedding and flying upward, mingling with the eagles in flight.

It was quiet. Very quiet.

Our daughter had taken her dad and grandfather's dream of

one day living in Alaska, and beat them to it. Our son's compass led him to Iowa. No more raucous laughter filled the house. No massive trips to the grocery store. No "can I borrow money for gas, Mom?" No more finding half-eaten Oreos™ and a clumpy, curdled, milk glass under a bed. No more mega loads of daily laundry to do, where one sock inevitably disappeared into a black hole or wherever missing or mismatched socks go.

I missed the kids terribly, but they were now adults. Bill and I remained steadfast to our promise to each other *and* the kids: advice was given only when *they* asked for it. Some of the calls from the kids came when they found themselves in a real predicament. The tone in their voice signaled desperation. They admitted they were overwhelmed and feeling anxious; finding themselves in financial trouble or major physical challenges of their own making. Many calls were for reassurance we still loved them, if we had confidence in them, and if we supported the decisions they were making. Sometimes the calls were to "toxic waste dump" or vent, *not* to get our advice. Then there were the times the kids just wanted someone to listen to them—and *not* speak. We learned the valuable lesson that the word *listen* has the same letters as *silent*.

Sometimes, silence *can* be golden.

It was not a simple task. We were grateful for the phone calls from the kids, no matter how sporadic they were. Bill and I often reminded each other we had given the kids deep roots. It was now time for them to fly on their own—even if they banged into a wall or two. And, like most twenty-somethings, they hit a few...hard. I fought the temptation to take the next flight to Alaska or Iowa to bail them out. Thankfully God reminded me my job was to pray and to let go and let *Him* deal with the situation. While we were with them in thought and prayer across the miles, this was now their season to discover that God never fails, nor is He ever late.

As I continued to watch the eagles soar on the thermals, I sighed. I was so glad both kids had a close, personal relationship and friendship with God and with each other as siblings. I reminded myself He numbered their days, and knew them long before I ever did. He had a plan and a purpose for their lives— plans to prosper them and not harm them. Plans for a hope and plans for their futures. I clung to Jeremiah 29:11 every time I prayed for them.

When God asked me to let go of my position at *Joni and Friends*™, I didn't realize how large the void left in my life would be. I thought Bill and I were headed for a ministry in respite and renewal, and not anything related to disability ministry.

I set my coffee down. In in the quiet of the moment, I picked up my journal.

I wrote the following in my journal:

"I believe the banner adage hanging in the WFTW™ office will be a large part of Joni's legacy. I know it will forever be written on my heart. The banner said:

'Disability ministry isn't disability ministry until the disabled are ministering.'

I wonder if Joni could ever imagine how God might use that fateful day in 1967 when she dove into the waters of Chesapeake Bay, hitting her head and becoming a quadriplegic, to pioneer and be on the cutting edge for international disability outreach, awareness, and ministry. God has used not only her story and testimony, but her humble, ever-tireless willingness and her utmost commitment to be used by Him."

Joni's willingness, hers (and Ken's!) commitment, have led to programs like *Family Retreat* (1991), *Wheels for the World* ™(1994), and the building of the *International Disability Center* (1997). In 2007, *The Christian Institute on Disability* was established to help train churches and communities world-wide, bringing awareness, practical assistance, and ideas for inclusion to share the Gospel around the world to the nearly one billion people who live with or are affected by disability. And that doesn't include the gazillion paintings, books, records, CD's, TV and radio programs she has done.

I ended my journal entry with the prayer: *"Lord, show me where You want me to minister."*

Within a year of leaving *Joni and Friends*™, both of my shoulders had to be rebuilt for a second time each. Rehabbing *one* shoulder is bad enough. But two shoulders? And throw a paralyzed diaphragm on top like a cherry?

I also had the first of many back surgeries. The damage was caused most likely from repeatedly doing what I told countless patients, family, and friends *not* to do, and the effects of DES exposure. Everything I knew and instructed others about posture, good body mechanics, and watching how much weight you lifted or carried (like fifty pound sacks of chicken feed) flew out the window when it came to taking care of myself.

On August 28, 2001, the 'biggie' hit.

We were getting ready for a Labor Day Weekend marathon of canning the fruits of our labor and bountiful garden. As I bent over to check the brine for the peaches, a sudden, explosive, and horrendously intense pain shot through my head. To this day, I can't find any other words to explain what it felt like. I have come to learn my explanation is an accurate description of what I was experiencing: a rare, active, three-compartment, subdural bleed of unknown origin.

It resulted in a one-way ticket to the hospital. After multiple scans, tests, and being poked and prodded, I was diagnosed as having a traumatic brain injury requiring intensive in-patient physical rehabilitation and nursing care. I did not return home for months. And Bill was left with the job to do all the canning

– solo.

During the long, lonely hours in the middle of the night in the rehab unit, I ever so slowly began to recognize God was answering the prayer I had journaled after I left *Joni and Friends*™. God *did* move me into the respite and renewal ministry. I just hadn't realized the journey included such a personal at-the-end-of-my-hand-*and*-medical/disability-ministry. It was becoming pretty obvious where my mission field was going to be: at hospitals and rehab centers, to doctors, nurses, surgeons, therapists, care-givers, and fellow sojourners on the path of learning how to live with chronic pain and long-suffering.

Sometimes I think I am going in the right direction, doing things the way God wants me to go... until I hear Him say to me, *"Care! Go right! No! No! Go the OTHER right—My right—not yours!"*

That's what I get for being a dyslexic disciple who sometimes gets things backwards or who forgets the admonishment of "be careful what you pray for—you just might get it!"

51

FAILURE IS NOT AN OPTION

The subdural brain bleed/traumatic brain injury was a last straw event for Bill.

He constantly worried about me. I couldn't be left alone as my poor coordination and balance issues made me a high fall risk. My speech was slow in returning. I spoke like Yoda, and on some days, my speech was reduced to acting out what I wanted to say – much like playing charades.

Bill and I were and are best friends. We were a team—but my half of the team couldn't keep up.

One Saturday night, three months after I had returned home from my in-patient rehab stay, Bill blurted out, "If you are going to die on me, Lady, you are going to die where we have been trying to get for over thirty years—Alaska."

Bill knew how much I loved living a carpenter's wife's dream: in a *completed* house. He saw how the accessibility amenities we designed and he built, made an immense difference as I was re-learning independent life skills. I was afraid to leave the comfort and safety of that house.

Bill told me he felt like he was betraying me, but felt like he was about to buckle under the heavy load of uncertainty that dawned each day with my neurological issues and stroke-like after-effects. The months of my being in a rehab facility, where he daily drove an hour each way to see me *and* working full-time was taking its toll—physically and emotionally. Thankfully, Bill and God were tight, talking often, sharing openly.

Bill never knew who he might wake up to. I had to re-learn how to walk, talk, and perform basic daily living skills as if I were a child. We knew the brain injury had most likely stripped my ability to work as an occupational therapist. I had to go on disability.

To cope, he did what he thought was best. He called his best friend in the world, Darrel. Bill said, "Get ready! You're going to help me drive and move us up to Alaska!

Without telling me, he quit his job. He put the house on the market. He sent me to stay with a friend, under the guise of getting a change of scenery. Then he arranged and packed our belongings up in a shipping container. On March 17, 2002, we headed north with our bare essentials packed into his pick-up truck and our little car.

In the truck, our Bouvier dog named Bo, and our talking cockatiel named Brattley, rode shot gun with Bill. Darrel and I followed in the car. We had a set of walkie-talkies to keep in touch between vehicles, since cell phone range was spotty. We were blessed as we drove with clear skies and roads, staying one day ahead of a heavy snowstorm.

Bill had no job waiting for him, but he knew what he knew— God had never failed us and He wasn't about to start. It didn't matter we were leaving against medical advice. Many people thought it was Bill who had suffered a head injury. They couldn't comprehend what seemed to them, a rash, selfish, and ludicrous decision.

What they failed to understand, was if anything was going to happen to me, Bill knew he needed to be by his little girl, now all grown up. It took a bit of time for our son to comprehend the gravity of his dad's decision. Nonetheless, Tim followed several years later, much to everyone's surprise and delight. The Tuk gang was together again.

To this day, Bill and I will say, "Moving to Alaska was the best decisions we ever made." (Well, second to our relationship to God and marrying each other… okay, *and* the kids.)

We live on an ideal piece of property with the Little Susitna River running through it. We can gaze at the Talkeetna Mountains and Government Peak —an area treasured for Alaskan hiking, skiing, dog-sledding, and a blueberry and mossberry picking mecca. It is also home to ginormous moose, bear, majestic eagles, marmots, ptarmigans and other native creatures.

The farm boy had come full circle. He had *finally* arrived where his father had so wanted to raise his family. Alaska.

His dad had modelled integrity and the importance of *both* voices being heard in a marriage. Bill's mom didn't want to raise four children under the age of five in the wilds and remoteness of Alaska while her husband was away working on the Alaska oil-pipeline or other construction jobs. Bill's parents were a true team, and his dad loved and esteemed his mom so highly, Bill's dad put *his* dream aside.

Bill had turned down several opportunities and offers to move to Alaska over the years. School, college sports scholarships, going to Nationals for wrestling, my internship at The Mayo Clinic, and later my health issues kept us in the Lower Forty-Eight. The day our daughter left for Alaska on a wing and a prayer, to live out a dream Bill had instilled in her was hard.

But Bill never let go of *his* dream, the desire of his heart, and unspoken prayer. He trusted God. Bill's faith, courage, and confidence prevailed. God never fails, and His timing is always perfect.

We arrived in Alaska on March 22, 2002.

52

YOU LIVE IN A WHAT?

When we first arrived in Alaska, with no job, no home, and full rehab mode for me, our daughter insisted we stay with her until we could get established. Bill found work right away, as superintendent of a project changing from sewage "ponds" to building a wastewater treatment facility.

We were blessed the job was only a fifteen-minute commute from our daughter's home. The civil engineers for the project were a brand-new firm. In fact, this was one of their first jobs. Once more, God had paved the way forward, as after the Wastewater Treatment project was completed, Bill was offered a job with the engineering firm. He became their Chief Inspector and "jack-of-all-trades" for fifteen years until his retirement.

We knew God had gone before us, with all the plans prepared. *HIS* plans – 20 acres including a river running through it, woods, hay field and garden, and a husband who could put it all together.

No, I didn't get a second dream house to go with our dream property. We *had* planned to build a smaller version of my dream house but got caught with an early first-week-in-October deep, hard freeze, followed by snow. The concrete company had to abruptly shut down for the winter early because of the weather, cancelling our scheduled foundation pour.

While *I* was sorely disappointed and worried—well, to be honest, more like having a panic attack about where we were going to live for the winter, it didn't faze Bill. He simply switched into his make-it-happen-mode. And make it happen he did.

Bill contacted a metal building contractor he'd met on the Wastewater Facility job. The contractor told Bill he had taken a custom order off his metal building supplier's hands as a favor—just one week before. Due to regulations the package couldn't be sold in the state originally purchased, so the supplier gave the contractor a ridiculously low price to take it. The contractor—you guessed it—gave Bill the same ridiculous (miraculous?) price for the package.

When he and Bill met to sign the paperwork, the contractor grinned and said, "Guess God's got *all* our backs on this one! I had *no* idea what I was going to do with it—especially with winter making an early appearance. It's a triple win!"

Bill couldn't agree more.

Within days, the contractor's company was erecting a 40x60 foot metal building on our property. Yep! We live in a metal building! Believe it or not, it is similar to the one we lived in when I returned from my internship in at The Mayo Clinic—without the horse stalls!

Originally, the plan was for the metal building to be Bill's shop with a small apartment and bathroom in it. We delayed the house-building plans until the following summer.

Insert one *long* pause and sigh!

However, Bill isn't one to sit around and do nothing. That winter he started working on various parts of the interior of the building. I often reminded him this was to be a *shop*—but he kept adding his signature amenities as he worked –things like pine ceilings and industrial grade carpeting; an office, a pantry, and large picture windows to watch the Northern Lights through. Bedrooms, a large kitchen, and of course an indoor bathroom completed his "shop".

Bill made it feel like a cozy, Alaskan cabin, where we dropped all our cares and troubles when we walked in the front door. We never did build a house. We found we loved living simply on our true slice of heaven on Earth piece of property. We are used to friends and visitors falling asleep on the couch in front of the woodstove. When they wake, we tell them we take it as a compliment they felt comfortable enough to drop their cares, to rest, and renew their soul.

Simplicity became our signature sign of sophistication. Less is more. As we have aged, we find there are few true *wants*, only our simple *needs*. Bill's love for cooking and gardening blossomed, as bountiful gardens and native plants on our property provided him the ingredients for new creative culinary delights along with jams, honey, spice blends, and more.

I cashed in my small retirement account from working in the schools and we purchased a 4x4 ATV with a bench seat, an enclosed cab, a 'dump box' bed and a winch on the front. Eventually we added a snow-plow to it. Many miles have been put on our 4x4, going to and from the river, driving around the acreage, and cleaning up debris as we landscaped our Alaskan home. While at one time I thought I always wanted to live in a real Alaskan log house, there is no way I'd trade my cozy cabin-like-feel home for the world.

Walking to and from the river became part of my daily regime. I spent hours down at an area we called Care's Corner, where the Little Susitna River meanders through out property. This was my special place to sit and meet with God. I basked in the warmth of His presence, reading books, or simply being still, mesmerized by the sound of the river. I spent hours looking for heart-shaped rocks or rocks with crosses on them. These times were therapy, too, restoring my broken body and soul from the many battles I had fought.

No matter where we have lived, no matter how many times we have moved (or God moved us!) our houses became homes. A place to drop troubles at the door, be embraced in the love of others, and warmed not only by the woodstoves, but the love our Heavenly Father has wrapped around us, keeping us safe—even on the raging battlefield called life.

53

REMEMBER YOUR SONG

My life battles continued to rage. Colon cancer and chemo sidelined me. Again.

A dear friend from out of state sent me a card. Somehow, cards, calls, or texts from her always came at the exact moment I needed to hear her calming voice and sage advice.

One day, I needed it more than I realized.

I called to thank her for the card and asked, "If I forget my song, my assignment in life, will you remind me of the tune?"

She chuckled and assured me saying, "Yes I will."

Several months passed. I called my friend again.

I told her—her card in my hand—I remembered what my song was, but I couldn't remember the tune. I was crushed. I was beaten down. I was weary. Totally void of any fight left in me. I felt I had lost my way. I paced around the house as I talked.

She listened and didn't say a word. She let me pour out my soul until I was empty and limp.

I shared how I was unaware of unintentionally hurting another close friend. I had forgotten the power words carry. Words we speak can be easily misconstrued, unintentionally.

My friend, who knew me possibly better than I knew myself, continued to listen not uttering a word. My gut wrenched and writhed in pain while I let it all out over the long-distance call— like spewing toxic waste all over her.

I spilled out my wrath and indignation as I paced through the house until my legs couldn't hold me any longer and I sat on the stairs.

I spit my irritation of not knowing who I'd be, or what level of function I had when I awoke each morning. I griped each day my body morphed into something I rarely recognized. Sags and bags replaced toned muscles. Glasses replaced once clear eyes. My bionic knees—filled with edema—resembled cantaloupes. The after effects of chemo neuropathy daily affect my feet. One day I might feel like I am walking on hot coals or sharp, pointed carpentry nails. The next day it might feel like my feet are freezing blocks of ice. The skin on my hands and feet continue to peel off every four to six weeks, often bleeding – a side effect that should have only lasted a month or two. I felt I was scarcely hanging on to the end of a severely frayed rope with barely a knot at the end. I wondered what about the outcome if I just let go.

The physically challenging hand I was dealt was more than a full house. My body is super-glued, titanium plated, remodeled, and bionic. Every fiber within me felt twisted, crunched, and distorted, but others couldn't see what I felt because it was all hidden and covered with skin. I might as well be relegated to the rag drawer for all it mattered.

I wailed to my friend on the phone, "No one gets it. *I* don't even get it."

I didn't *look* like I had a disability or that I battle to stay alive.

She listened to me as I whined, admitting my husband was right...again.

Bill had been trying to help me come to acceptance of the hand dealt to me. God in His infinite wisdom had allowed us to go through all these trials for some reason. And even though I didn't understand it—this was my body's new normal. I had a body with multiple hidden disabilities, and it fought multiple battles simultaneously.

After she listened to my tirade, my friend talked me through it all. She knew I needed to take some time to rediscover my Life-Song. The song God had breathed into me when I was born. I needed to re-work some of the measures and melodies and pay more attention to the rests, not just the loud crescendos. Yes, my life, my body wasn't predictable. It was always changing. My Life-Song needed to reflect that.

As her words washed over me, I took a breath and paused. I realized the song *I* was focusing on was not the song *God* had written for me. My focus was not on the tune where the measures flowed easily. Instead, I'd allowed anger to rise on days when I awoke to unfamiliar *me*. My 'baditude' showed up when I couldn't do what *I* physically wanted to do. The task had to be left for someone else to do, which made me cringe even more. There were days I literally didn't know if I was capable of continuing on.

I sat crumpled on the stairs, my cheeks streaked with tears. My breath came in gulps. My friend continued to silently listen. It seemed like the phone line was dead as neither of us spoke.

With slow and stiff movements, I stood up. I looked at the mountains outside our living room window. As if on cue, Big One—the name we'd given to one of our favorite eagles—soared to the heavens on a thermal updraft.

Strangely, I began to hear not only my song, but the tune. Some of the words were missing. No... they weren't missing, they were rearranged. In their place was a pause—a rest. Vaguely, I remembered something from when I took piano lesson days as a child. A *rest* is an important part of the music.

Exhausted and worn, I had been rebelling against a body I had little control over. I thought I had come to the end of my song. Instead, what my song needed was for me to not ignore the *rest*. I couldn't disregard the pause if I wanted to make my tune flow. It needed to create a time for healing and *not* just for me.

I *know* my song. I *know* the tune. While the battle-worn arrangement might need a *wee* bit more tweaking and practice, I know my song can and will soar to the heavens, carried on a thermal updraft to the One who created my song.

What about *your* song?

54

HAVE YOU TAKEN YOUR VITAMIN B3 TODAY?

How I act or react to any given situation or in any given daily life battle is a choice. And, my choice will affect not just me, but those I interact with throughout each day. One tactic I use is to choose by starting each morning taking a dose of Vitamin B3.

"Vitamin B3?" You might ask. "I've never heard of it. Is it part of a Super B Vitamin Complex?"

"Nope!" I smiled. "Vitamin B3 stands for *Bible Before Breakfast* or *Beyond Brokenness Blessings*." I find spending quiet time, reading His Word in the Bible and several devotional books calms me and prepares me for whatever I might face.

I have come to learn trouble, tough times, and heavy sieges rarely come to someone without leaving them a nugget of gold in their hand.

There have been blessings too numerous to count that have come my way. I might never have received them had I not been willing to accept and endure the suffering throughout my life. I think of the people I have met, the friendships I have made both near and far; the authors I have been introduced to and their books I have read in the midst of a a season of suffering or being set aside, to recuperate or steer clear from the pandemic germ warfare.

I have a friend, when they enter a room, every nook and cranny fills with joy. They exude and radiate *contagious* joy. It is a delight to watch the joy wash over the room.

My friend's entire family—from their sidekicks, their kids, in-laws, nieces, nephews, siblings—the whole kit and caboodle possess what I call the "joy gene." When you come into their presence, you are welcomed as if you were the most important person they know. Big grins spread across their face and you can be assured an accompanying hug is not far behind. When I am in their presence or chatting with one of them, I find *my* heart grows in size and a smile breaks out so big my cheeks hurt. This family knows no stranger.

One could never guess in a million years the battles, the adversities, and challenges on multiple fronts that have chiseled and molded their souls. Even on days when they were running on empty, when their hearts were shattered and they felt totally broken inside, they chose to let their joy gene emanate and be poured out. Their words to a fellow man or woman are filled with honest, true compassion. Nary do you leave their presence without feeling encouraged. It's no wonder they are known as pillars of the communities they each live in.

This family reminds me one of my favorite stories in the Bible. It is the story of a woman who, in all of her brokenness, in all of her desolation, poured out a treasured and lavish jar of perfume over the feet of Jesus. The woman was at the end of her proverbial rope. She felt dejected, not to mention rejected by the townspeople. She felt crushed, beaten down, overwhelmed from any direction she turned. Yet, with unabashed joy, she gave her all—the finest, the very best of what she had.

At first, people were aghast at what they saw happening. Did she not know the cost of what she was doing? The fragrance emanating from the broken and poured out jar began to fill the room. Its essence trickled in the air, seeping through each and every crack and crevice. The precious scent wafted and gently settled upon each person, eventually permeating their clothes. Those witnessing this incredible occurrence realized something no words could explain. Something remarkable was happening.

A sweet spirit of release and peace settled over the room. A sense of gratitude was released, as if each person was personally unshackled from the chains of their daily burdens. No longer did the enormous burden of their challenges and adversity they carried deep within weigh them down.

Yes, this pouring out and even the brokenness came at great expense—for the woman in the story pouring the perfume out, as well as my friend and their family thousands of years later. But they both had counted the cost. They willingly made a choice. Enter Vitamin B3.

They do not let the burdens, the shackles, the desolation, the disappointment, or the daily challenges buffeting them from every which way define who they are. They are willing to courageously be broken and poured out. The life they live and the choices they make are evident to others. Even when weeping endures through many of their long-suffering nights, their joy gene arises in the morning. Their joy is reflected in who they are and are called to be. They choose to let go and let God. Because of their faith and daily walk with God, they each know their weeping will turn to joy and will be contagious.

Life will continue to be a daily battle, doling out challenges, obstacles, and disappointments. But we have a choice in how we handle it. Will you be like my friend, and today, with reckless abandon, be willing to be broken and poured out? Will you allow your brokenness to change not only *your* countenance, but possibly the countenance of each person you encounter, as you share your joy and compassion?

Many of the joys I have experienced could only come after I walked courageously through many sorrows. I have come out stronger after each battle, even though I bear the scars and weariness from the fight.

Life *is* hard. But God is good. All the time. Sometimes you just have to dig deep, trusting and knowing: God never fails and His timing is perfect.

55

WATER WATER EVERYWHERE – ALASKA STYLE

The Little Susitna River meanders and cuts through our acreage, so we own property on both sides of the river. After our former flood experiences, we *thought* we were prepared for the possibility of flood waters rising.

We knew about winter ice dams (and beaver dams!), and over-flows occur when ice melts then re-freezes, often raising the water level. We found out our error was thinking when the waters of the Little Su (as the locals call it) rise, it would likely be during Spring break-up when the snow melts and the ground finally thaws. But nooo…of course not.

The three floods we have experienced, all six years apart, have come during the August-early-September rainy season. Each flood brought their own set of challenges and debris aftermath.

In 2006, the Little Su was serenely meandering around Care's Corner and down the main channel. In mere moments it became a roaring, furious monster. I dared to take a step outside. The winds were howling over seventy miles per hour, while the rain fell at a rate of more than an inch an hour.

The cracking sound of trees as they snapped made the noise similar to the volley of semi-automatic gunfire. The splintered trees were thrown into the raging waters as it rose higher and higher. Even majestic hundred-year-old cottonwood trees became causalities as they were torn from their roots, and tumbled into the muddy mix of water.

A month prior to the flood, my diaphragm had become paralyzed after a rare, shoulder surgery complication, necessitating being on oxygen. Thankfully, my monthly supply of oxygen and extra tanks had been delivered before roads became impassable. The stress of the situation compounded my need for extra oxygen.

While I knew Bill was on his way home, it brought little comfort, as the news reported on the various closed roads—or were quickly becoming closed, submerged or even collapsed. Some roads were totally washed away as the angry, rolling water rose higher and higher. Our road was likely be added to the list, since we had to cross a bridge over the rising water of the Little Su. It is the only egress for the families who live on our road.

Tears of relief ran down my face as I saw Bill's truck headlights coming down our driveway. At the same moment, the news reported our road had indeed flooded and was closed to all traffic. Then we lost power.

The emergency service agency in our Borough know which families have medical issues and what the medical needs are, if evacuation became necessary. Alaska is unique in contrast to other places we lived in the way they organize people, band resources together, and make a point to know the needs of people *before* a disaster hit.

Log jams and debris piled up, blocking the main channel. The river ox-bowed, totally changing the direction the river flowed. Several feet of rock were deposited at what once was Care's Corner. It buried our barbeque, took out our storage hut where we kept camp chairs and picnic supplies. The force of water took out the foot bridge Bill had built so we could watch salmon as they made their way upstream to spawn.

The river usually ran two hundred feet or more from the actual house. Knowing we were in the one-hundred-year flood plain,

Bill had built in extra protection, building our house more than ten feet above specifications, just to be sure. Even so, the water rose so high at one point, we could watch wayward salmon outside our bedroom window. It gave us a whole new meaning to "river-front property."

When the rain stopped, we ventured out in our hip boots to see the aftermath. News reports reached us of a house upstream from us had been washed away. Their freezer, a couch, clothing, and a large propane tank now resided in the debris mess at what was Care's Corner. Acres of our hay had sloughed off, revealing river bedrock. The main channel of the river no longer ran in front of homes down river from us, leaving neighbors with a gravel yard instead.

In 2012, we experienced our second Alaskan flood. We not only lost another barbeque and fire pit, but we lost numerous trees and the land that was our main ATV and walking trail. And this time… Care's Corner was obliterated. It was no more.

We had no way to get to the other side of our property. The main channel of the river had changed course once again, boring a wide path, previously a small gulley. No water flowed anywhere near where Care's Corner used to be.

The loss of my special place where I went for respite and renewal was devastating to me. When the floodwaters subsided, the flat surface of my walking trail was replaced with a boulder field. With my bionic knees and balance issues, the only time I could safely walk over the large boulder field was in the winter, after several feet of snow had fallen and I could traverse across wearing my snowshoes. Even driving over the boulder field in the Ranger was physically painful on my surgically fused back.

I cried out in anger to God when I saw the aftermath and what it did to my once calm, peaceful, serene, piece of heaven we called *Care's Corner*. I literally cried. I cried in bodily pain and mental anguish every time I walked out to the river. My loss ran deeper than the river itself. My anger at God ran even deeper, and I let Him have an earful on more than several occasions.

The wrath of the flood deposited seven, one-hundred-year-old cottonwood trees and their humongous root wads right smack dab in the middle of my once pristine corner. The tree trunks across the river were entangled in brush and debris three feet high. I cried and vowed to never forgive God. I could not see how beauty could return after such devastation.

Yet as the saying goes, "time has a way of healing." It took me a couple years, but I finally reconciled my anger with God over how-dare-He-take-my-special-place away and all the trees lining my walking paths? After all, the property was only on loan to us temporarily in this life. While I still didn't understand the why, I conceded it *was* His land to remodel the way He saw fit.

The healing time brought to me? It wasn't the removal of the ugly trees, or the massive boulder field disappearing, or even the return of the river to its former route. The healing came with my vision and how I looked at things. Oh, I still cry, missing Care's Corner on occasion, but slowly, my eyes were filled with wonder.

If I were in God's shoes, I'm not so sure I could have been as patient with this dyslexic disciple, waiting for me to stop being angry and go out and discover the new wonders and treasures He left for me: the wonder at the new deep pools of clear glacial water; at how the salmon responded and found new spawning areas or how the eagles perched majestically on the ugly root wad in the middle of the river—the tree where they used to nest. We found a new sandy beach in a carved-out cove where little ones could play safely away from the rivers' current. The floods left millions of rocks, each with their own unique, intricate pattern. Wonder at the resiliency of nature—like new spruce trees growing out of a jumbled mess of grass, weeds, and left-over debris. Wonder at how I could have even *thought* of being mad at God. Wonder at forgiveness…both mine and God's toward me.

In August 2018, the heavens opened up once again. Water flowed over the one egress closing the road again to all but tall pick-up trucks. Not even school buses were allowed to go through the water, for as long as there was water flowing over it, there were safety concerns of the road washing out. More trees were ripped from their roots, the log debris floating down the river, looking like a jammed up starting line of a marathon race.

We could only wait and watch as nature once again remodeled our property. More of our hay field sloughed away. At one point, the volume of water was so high it ran through all of the prior main channels. Once the flood water receded and we could assess the damage, we found we had not only lost more trees, we gained more river-rock property.

The river now runs about one hundred feet from the house. The way it is flowing, it is slowly undercutting the banks and the trees left standing at river's edge.

When heavy rains are in the forecast, I no longer fear the worst. We are flood and emergency ready. The neighborhood co-op communications and provision supplies are readied. Our faith and courage secure, we wait and watch, having front row seats to one of nature's wonders. We know God's love will guide and protect us… and Bill can always build us an ark, if necessary!

56

COME OUT, COME OUT WHEREVER YOU ARE

One of my favorite things about living where we do in Alaska is having a front row seat to watching the Northern Lights.

I have book-marked **https://www.gi.alaska.edu/monitors/aurora-forecast** so I can watch both the weather and aurora forecasts to hopefully catch a glimpse. It is a bit like playing cat and mouse. While a higher number to see the Auroras is best, some of our best viewings have been when the number has been as low as a number two on the scale. We can see the Auroras from September to March, sometimes later—it all depends on the timing and light and solar flares.

This is what a night is like when I have been blessed to see them:

The first evening stars tentatively blink. The pale sky turns dark. A few more candle-lit stars flit and twinkle on. A wide, sweeping wind hints of a chilly winter coming. The Milky Way curves across the fully announced night. Suddenly, a light pulses over the majestic bald head of a mountain peak. The Auroras! The pulse gets stronger. Purple, green, white, and red colors weave and wildly dance across the night sky. Suddenly, they fade and are gone.

As I continue looking out the window I can't resist going outside. My feet, clad in summer socks, ache from the cold, hard concrete I stood on. I become dizzy as I crane my neck backward, mesmerized with the hope of seeing more of the wandering show of Northern Lights.

My wait is rewarded. This time the lights are more green and white. As the Auroras pulse across the sky, I see the shapes of animals. There's an eagle! There's a salmon! There's a polar bear! There's a raven! I witness the lore of tales told by Native elders.

Once again, the lights disappear and the sky returns to its star-studded state. After ten minutes I sigh and retreat back into the house. Plus my feet are cold!

I decidedly plop myself in front of the fire and bury myself in pillows and a cozy comforter. I settled in for an evening game of watching for the Auroras to appear again. I am ever hopeful I might glimpse the elusive place where the lights meet the sky and the land and the sea. It is the place where colors dance with the wild wind; where the tame breezes and lucky few people dance and rejoice over the wild and wonderful waves of color fills our very soul.

I gaze up into the silence of the night and watch for any signs through the living room windows.

I pray, *"Lord, the Auroras are Your handiwork at its best. How grateful I am to be able to take in this canvas, in the warmth of my own home, in the peace we enjoy, protected by a country and brothers and sisters who are willing to make it so. Help me to never take these moments for granted. Help me to never get so involved or be so busy I can't take a moment to stop and drink in Your most precious sights. If I do, please remind me what Life is really about. And Lord... Thanks."*

I pull the comforter tighter; I rub my eyes and let out a long yawn. My eyes become heavy laden with sleep. I glance out the window to see the colorful lights appear again—dancing for a brief moment, then gone. It's a forever reminder to be like the lights. Be all you are, inside and out, even in your dreams under the Midnight Sun.

When was the last time you went outside just to stare at the stars before you slipped into dreamland?

57

I'M IN ENERGY CONSERVATION MODE

I am frequently asked, "With all you've gone through, what is your secret to on how to stay so positive when things keep going so bad?"

While I have no one pat answer, I usually turn to humor. It's a lesson I've learned from life and life-long friends.

I might say, "That's the way the pickle squirts! Sometimes sweet, sometimes dill, and often times not kosher—even though I feel like I'm being chopped into relish at the moment."

Or I might reply, "Actually, I'm just in energy conservation mode—it takes more muscle power and energy to pout and frown than laugh and smile."

Then there is my husband's favorite, "No pain, no gain! Think of all you are gaining!" (Thanks for the encouragement, sweetheart!)

Humor has been a staple in our marriage—from the campfire scene in Blazing Saddles™ and other funny movies, to the primitive salt-box sitting on our hutch that reads: "I'm not arguing – I'm just explaining why *I'm* right!"

I particularly like the metal wall hanging on the the stairwell wall: "Trespassers Will Be Composted" or the one hanging next to it, "If a man is in his garden, alone, is he still wrong?" (Seriously? You want *me* to answer that last one?!)

I have been buoyed when friends send me funny cards, raising my endorphin level, known to aid in healing and good health. I especially loved the card: "A nurse asked me: on a scale of 1-10, 1 being low and 10 being high, how do you rate your pain? I responded: That is a rookie scale—do you have one for experts?" Of course it came on a day when my pain level was at a fourteen-plus!

I have several who use humor in their cancer outreach support groups, their medical practice or at their job—using humor to deal with life's tough times—whether a job loss, an illness or tragic episode, to bullying, suicide, or post-traumatic stress from battling for our country's freedom in front of audiences of all ages, world-wide.

Christine Clifford has facilitated *The Cancer Club: Humorous and Helpful Products for People with Cancer.* Linda Hawes Clever, MD, MACP is founding President of RENEW a not-for-profit aimed at helping devoted people maintain (and regain) enthusiasm, effectiveness, and purpose. David Naster, founder of YJHTL, (You Just Have To Laugh) writing, speaking and cruising through the many bodies of water making earth a special place to live on. David is one of the *only* clean, reverent, ethical comedians I have ever heard. He holds audiences captive using humor to hit and heal the hard places of our heart and soul that many of us willingly don't dare explore. His books and YouTube segments have been valuable and helpful, too.

I am blessed to have mentors and friends as these, who can tickle my funny bone, making me laugh until I cry tears of pent-up grief that end up turning into tears of joy. I have included their information in the resource section, at the end of the book. I hope you will spend time exploring their sites and recommendations.

Humor helps us to heal. It is free for all of us to use, there is no co-pay or deductible, and we can use it as often as we want.

So…what are you waiting for?

58

SPOILER ALERT:
THERE IS NO "NORMAL" IN ALASKA

"What do I do? What do I do?" I shrieked into the telephone to my husband. "It's not stopping!" I screamed, as the bed heaved and the chest of drawers moved back and forth.

On the other end of the phone call, Bill pulled his truck off to the side of the road. He started laughing. "Dang, my work truck is even shaking! This *is* a good one!!"

"The inside chimes are going crazy! It's not stopping! Do I run outside or stay sitting on the bed? Never mind! I'm **not** staying in the house." I slammed the phone down. Right then our one hundred thirty pound Mastiff/Ridgeback mix dog, Bubba Grump, came bounding in, his slobber swinging side to side and jumped up on the bed with wild eyes, as if to say, "what is happening?!"

Jumping out of bed, I grabbed my bathrobe and slippers and ran out in my skivvies and bare feet, *not* taking the time to put them on until I got outside. Our neighbor, who lived several acres away, came running full speed to check on me. She too, was pulling clothes haphazardly on. The earth finally stopped moving. We held each other tight for a few more minutes.

Suddenly she shrieked loudly and firmly grabbed onto me. A 6.4 after-shock began to shake the ground beneath our barely clad feet, bouncing and jostling us as we tried to gain our balance and wits. Poor Bubba, confused, was trying to stay on all fours.

After the two of us were reasonably sure the worst had past, she went home, and I went back inside. I called Bill, still shaking from what had just happened.

Bill told me to settle down, and to check if I saw anything major askew. Books had fallen off shelves, and two telephone glass insulators and an over 70 year old one-quart-glass milk jug had fallen from their eight-foot-high window ledge, leaving glass on the floor and carpet. Oddly, a one-hundred-fifty-year-old sterling silver kerosene lamp of my grandmother's, and has a *very* thin glass chimney, was lying on its side, next to the broken insulator and milk jug. It had fallen off the shelf at the same height as the other broken items, but it had no damage on it. Not a ding or chip.

Next, I went into my office. Once there, I discovered three of my Willow Angels® had fallen, but did not break. The two angels whose hands were clasped in prayer lay at either end of a wooden plaque that had also fallen. The plaque said: "Life is Fragile. Handle with Prayer." How apropos…and actually amusing.

The news reported it was a 7.1 magnitude earthquake. We ended up having over 8,000 aftershocks in the month after the quake. One might think since we knowingly live on a fault line in the "Ring of Fire," plus being aware Alaska has dozens of earthquakes a week, I would be used to the shakers. To be honest, we rarely notice an earthquake unless they have a magnitude of 4.5 or over. We stir our coffee in 3.5's!

When the quake was shaking for what seemed forever, I became more than shaken. I became grateful I was not my son, who, at the moment, was working on one of Alaska's main highways, about fifteen miles from the epicenter of the quake, on a survey crew. I was grateful Bill was not on the twisted, mangled road headlining national news. Some sections of the road had disappeared into oblivion. He had driven over it ten minutes before the quake hit. I was blessed to receive the call our daughter and her family were all safe, as was their house. They lived only a mile from the epicenter. Other homes in their neighborhood were not as fortunate, nor were several schools and businesses nearby. They had to be completely rebuilt.

As I continued to take inventory around the house I noticed several pictures in the house were a bit crooked, and several small things had moved, but nothing major.

Then, about thirty minutes after the quake, I heard an unusual chime sound. It chimed nine times. I'd never heard the sound before. While we do have a clock collection, none of the chimes are activated. With a heart loudly pounding, I cautiously made my way upstairs. Low and behold, a German cuckoo clock from my husband's grandparents, which had not worked in well over forty years, was tick-toking away! The time had been stuck at 8:30 ever since we inherited it, some thirty years earlier. So the nine chimes I heard? Yep! Nine o'clock!!

We laughed at the reaction of the reporters and people in the Lower forty-eight. They were amazed there were no fatalities. The picture of the buckled and blown apart road Bill had been on just before the earthquake was fixed in three days. Crews from all over the local area pitched in. The road construction/repair season was well over, so crews were available. Since the already shut-down-for-the-season asphalt plant had to be fired back up again, the road took longer than originally hoped for.

A friend from the southern part of the United States called to check on us. With a chuckle in her voice she said, "If that had been back here it would've taken three months to three years to get something done. First we'd have to have to wait for a steering committee to be formed, then we'd have dozens of public hearings, and still no decisions would have been made. Y'all up there in Alaska just aren't normal. Y'all just fix it!"

I agreed with her and replied, "Pretty much!"

What else were we supposed to do? Only twenty percent of the state is on a road system. The featured road on the news is heavily used. We did what Alaskans do—take care of each other and take care of what needs to be done—together.

While we may not be "normal," we do what needs to be done—together.

59

ON THE GROUNDS OF GRIEF

The last couple of years have been filled with harsh lessons of tough love and lessons of unquestionable trust. We experienced a shattered brokenness we knew could only be allowed by God Himself. I had an overwhelming temptation to ask, "*Why*, God?" Bill lovingly said it was futile to ask "why" or even "why now?" It was above our pay grade. God would answer – all in His time.

Our world was jolted when we received a call on June 24, 2019. Our son-in-law, through his sobs, told us our precious and long-prayed for daughter, unexpectedly passed away. She was twenty-three weeks pregnant with a baby girl, and was the mother to our two "toe-mater sandwich-makers," ages two and four at the time.

She had been up in the early morning hours, propped up on the couch, snuggled under her favorite blanket (with a broken leg, no less). She was searching "heartburn" on her computer. Heartburn pestered her during her second trimester with both our incredible grandson, and our pretty-princess granddaughter.

When the medical examiner told her husband the cause of death, he simply said, "It was just her time to go." He told her husband *nothing* could have been done, by *anyone*. Even if she had been in the hospital, no one could have done anything. No MRI, no test available could have prevented the cause of death. The medical examiner said she died quickly and without pain or warning. It wasn't a clot from her broken leg surgery, it wasn't being pregnant, or problems with the baby, or her heart valve transplant ten years prior...nothing. Her large heart—always putting everyone and everything before herself, just stopped beating. His words brought great comfort at a time we were in the deep, surreal pain of loss and grief.

As we prepared for our daughter's Celebration of Life, God showed up in ways only He could. Alaska was in the middle of experiencing a historic heat wave. Several large and devastating fires were burning in the region, leaving a thick smoky haze hanging heavily in the air. It depleted everyone's stamina and endurance, much less having to deal with grief. It *never* gets to ninety degrees where we live!

Two days before the memorial service, the families needed a break. A break from making the memorial plans, attending to the many details surrounding the death of a loved one, the enormity of the situation, the heat, and a break from each other. We all needed a day of rest.

I went down to our river for respite and renewal. I sat for hours. I went to one of my favorite spots—partially to keep cool, partially to be still and to listen. I was also hoping to find the right words to share about the incredible daughter, sister, wife, mother, and friend Jamie was.

I lost track of time as the lull of the river meandered in front of me. A light, cool breeze blew through the stately trees across the river from where I was sitting. The breeze allowed the emotions and exhaustion from the frenetic pace we had been keeping to float away. Peace surrounded me as I sat. Sweet Peace.

It Is Well, written by Horatio Spafford, is one of my favorite hymns. Sorrow like sea billows had been rolling. Losing my daughter with whom I was so close was incomprehensible—and I know it will be until we are reunited in Heaven. But sitting down by the river with my mug of iced coffee made it easier.

The last gift Jamie had given me just a month earlier for Mother's Day was the coffee mug I held in my hand. The mug said, "It is well with my soul" – the words in the refrain of the hymn. She had filled the coffee mug with packets of my favorite blend of coffee. She and I *loved* our coffee! It was as if God knew I needed a tangible something to hang onto in the days ahead when I actually couldn't hang onto or hug my daughter. Yes, it *was* well with my soul, even though my heart ached. I headed back up to the house, knowing I would need every bit of that peace in the days ahead.

We spent the next day visiting with close friends and family who congregated at the kids' house. We busied ourselves arranging and rearranging things here and there, making sure everything was ready for the Celebration of Life. We played hopscotch, hide-and-seek and played tag with our two grandkids and their many cousins—all who had plenty of energy to spare and filled with over-flowing joy.

It was easy to lose track of time as it was summer solstice week, with close to twenty hours of sunlight. Before we realized it, it was after 9:00p.m.—it was no wonder I was so worn out! I'm no spring chicken!

We drove the forty miles home in silence, both tired and with little to say. We were discovering grief has a way of knocking the stuffing out of you. Sometimes there are no words to say—even to each other. When we arrived home, I lumbered out of our truck. As I was closing the truck door, I heard a loud, crashing noise. It sounded like it was nearby. I asked Bill what he thought the noise was.

"Oh, it's probably just something next door," he replied as he wearily walked towards the front door of our house.

The next morning, July 1st, was the day of the Celebration of

Life. Bill went outside early, to water the garden. The heat wave continued. It was already 72 degrees at 7 a.m. We were blessed that a slight breeze had cleared the prior days of thick, hazy and smoky skies caused from area forest fires.

I still didn't know what words I was going to share at the service. Propped up and positioned with pillows around me on my adjustable hospital bed that often doubles as my comfortable writing or reading spot, I sipped my morning coffee.

My thoughts were abruptly interrupted when Bill rushed into the room and breathlessly said, "Quick! Grab your cell phone! I don't have time to grab my good camera, and I don't want to miss it! You've *got* to see what's in the sky!"

I ran out as quickly as I could. When I got outside, Bill pointed upward. I looked to where he was pointing.

"Look at that..." He could barely choke out the words. Tears tricked down his cheeks.

Overhead in the clear, robin blue sky was one cloud formation. One. It was in the shape of a cross. On the left arm of the cross was the shape of an eagle feather. Tears continued to stream down Bill's cheeks. We silently held each other's hand. Ever since Jamie was little, one of our strong bonds with her was eagles. I snapped a couple photos.

I softly said, "I think God's saying to us: *"It's going to be alright, guys. She's in Good Hands."*

Wiping his eyes, Bill said to me, "We have to walk down to the river, too. You won't believe what I have to show you."

Once at the river, I looked at the scene before me. Bill was right. I *couldn't* believe my eyes. There, lying *across* the river was one of the enormous birch trees keeping me cool only two days prior. My camp chair was buried beneath the limbs and leaves. I stood there, dazed, thinking about what could have been. I turned to Bill and said, "I think that's my warning sign of what *not* to say at the service!

I looked upward and said, "Message received! Pinky Promise! I won't tell *that* story about you!" Deep within, I knew things would be okay.

We walked up to the house, tightly holding hands. While we knew the day was going to be hard, we knew *Who* held the day... and our daughter and baby girl.

60

CELEBRATING LIFE

The Celebration of Life was just that. Tears were shed, stories were told, and laughter inter-mingled with the tears. Our son informed all attending how Jamie's love ran deep. He shared how his sister, (unbeknownst to us,) slept on the floor next to his bed, every night for the first month after we adopted him, to help him know he was safe and didn't need to be afraid of the dark. He also shared the unknown tale of how she had shot compressed air up his nose when they were cleaning their laptops.

And, he shared more—from her speeding tickets, to burned-up clutches as she taught him how to drive a stick-shift vehicle; her sage love and life advice she had given him. He shared it wasn't going to be easy going forward without his sister, but he promised to take her advice: "Don't make it more than it was; and don't make it any less than it was." Most importantly," he said, "he would remember to see the best in himself and others, because she found the best in him."

He finished by promising he will strive to live with the values she embraced: An unyielding faith that kept her family strong; boundless love for her family and friends; and the hope her kids will be able to see *her* love reflected through him.

When it was my turn to share, I felt a total peace settle over me. I knew it was from God—a Peace passing all understand-ing—especially in that excruciating moment. It was far from easy to put into words all my daughter was to me.

How can I share without dissolving into tears? I wondered to myself.

God's peace and grace prevailed. Afterward, people asked how could I get up and share—so calm, so collected, so real. I told them there was only one way. It was God.

I began by sharing life had never been easy for Jamie. She never knew me a day without cancer. Yet the day her true soul-mate walked into her life, it became the BEST day, and for the rest of her life—and ours, too. We gave her hand in marriage to her husband, to cleave to him and him to her, and to put *their* family first. We knew they were in Good Hands—God's. And they *did* cleave to each other and put their little family first.

To those who knew Jamie knew she was graceful, beautiful and caring in every way. She put others before herself, almost to a fault. Her twinkling chameleon-colored eyes and giggle always lit up a room.

I shared with those attending her Celebration of Life, watching her with the late Senator Ted Stevens, one of the longest serving Senators in history, was more than special. We were in the Strom Thurmond Room at the U.S. Capitol Building in Washington, D.C. The two of them were looking down at the Jefferson Memorial, quietly talking about what it was like to be a daughter of a parent battling cancer—just like she and his daughter had been.

She represented Corporate Fred Meyer/Kroger™ well in Washington D.C., sharing with various Senators (in their lunch room, no less!) how important cancer research funds were needed. She called the Senate Subway cars "Willie Wonka Cars" as they took us and the rest of the delegation from Alaska from one place to another.

I shared, just days earlier, I had found and re-read the letters Jamie had written to us when she was at Basic Training Boot

Camp for the Coast Guard. In her last letter she wrote: "God has been with me every step of the way. He has shown me He has great plans for me—even after the Coast Guard. I'm so glad and hope you are proud of me."

She was right – God *did* have big plans for her: to become an incredible wife and amazing mother. We were *more* than proud of her.

Even so, she was *so* "her daddy's "Little Girl—her father's daughter." It was clearly shown on her Father's Day present. They were the last words he heard from his baby girl, printed on a primitive salt box that arrived three days after she died. It said: "You are my favorite pain in the ass…" (They had special father/daughter bond that, yes, sigh…even included a few salty, yet always used jokingly, names they would call each other.)

Stubborn, independent, a confidant *and* confident; she could fix things and make them better. She was strong and fearless—even showing people how to jump out of helicopters on heli-skiing adventures in remote parts of Alaska. She asked her *DAD* to take her shopping for her *Junior Miss Pageant* ball gown. (You can tell what she thought of *my* fashion sense!)

The words to the song *Butterfly Kisses*™ (Bob Carlise) fit our daughter to a "T." Jamie was sent down from Heaven—she *was* Daddy's little girl. She gave her dad butterfly kisses each night after she said her bedtime prayers and he helped saddle her pony, Pal, while she had little white flowers from our hayfield, all up in her hair. Bill sang the song to her and with her, often. Tears flowed long and hard as they danced together to the song once last time, at her wedding in November 2013.

She was my "go-to" girl-friend, besides daughter—something we both treasured. She called me almost every weekday morning at *exactly* 9:38—on her way to work, to run errands, pre-school or play-dates. We talked and texted often—when we were happy, sad, or mad, or just to let off steam about life in general. She'd *always* close with "I love you, Mom."

I replied, "Love you s'mores!"

I continued to share how I will miss her gourmet cooking, especially her Triple Fudge Brownie *Bailey's*™ cheesecake. I just wish she hadn't taken her "secret tweak" to her raspberry jam recipe with her to Heaven...it's *not funny*! (Well, maybe a little bit...sort of...*not really*!)

Those who are walking or who have walked the journey of grief *know* it is not something you "get over." One gets "through it." The Almighty is holding us up, our friends are surrounding us, and we have a daily resolve to put one foot in front of the other, taking one day at a time.

Just as God counts the number of hairs on our head (or the lack there-of!) we know He numbers each of our days. We know our daughter and baby girl are in Good Hands. I expect to see them dancing up a storm, sliding on the Aurora's as they shimmer and shine above us.

61

DOES JOB HAVE A SISTER?

As if I didn't have enough medical nuts, bolts and screws holding my body together, days after returning from my first book tour in the Lower forty-eight in 2011, for *Loose Screws and Skinned Knees*, another incident wreaked a bit more havoc. I was on my way to deliver books to our local hospice.

As I stepped out of the car, I slipped on a teensy-tiny patch of left-over April Alaskan ice. The palm of my right hand took the full-force of my weight as I fell. Due to post-chemo side effects, plus other DES bone issues, I ironically fractured my *upper* arm— my humerus bone, to be exact. After another surgery, I became the proud, new owner of an upper-arm-plate and *ten* new screws.

Unfortunately, eight years later, and two short weeks after Jamie's Celebration of Life, the arm hardware started failing. Several screws were beginning to damage the upper arm muscle and starting to protrude through the humerus, making it necessary to surgically remove the hardware, as soon as possible. While I was elated removing the plate and ten screws out would let me be "less screwed up," my jubilation was short lived.

The plan was to put in a reverse total shoulder with a long titanium rod giving my arm stability and hopefully more function and less pain. Prior to surgery I joked with the orthopedic surgeon, reminding him who he was working on and asked him if he had a Plan B just in case. We chuckled as I counted backward breathing in the anesthesia.

During surgery, complications *did* arise. After removing the plate and screws, it was discovered I had no deltoid muscle—the key muscle needed for the intended surgical procedure of replacing the plate and screws with a reverse total shoulder.

The surgeon told me after the surgery he was glad he actually had a Plan B. Several physician friends of his had teased him when they saw my name on the surgical calendar with his name as the surgeon and told him he was either nuts or brave. Or both!

During the surgery, he had to swiftly switch gears, determining the best (and only) option was to put in a *regular* total shoulder, with an extra-long titanium rod, to protect the voids where the hardware had been.

Surgery went three hours longer than expected. Consequently, I lost a great deal of blood. The plan of my going home that day was crushed. I spent the day after surgery receiving several units of blood. I joked with the nurses, saying they should just send me to Jiffy-Lube®—it'd be less expensive!

The hits kept coming.

Hours after the blood transfusions, I had a reaction. The life-saving transfusion given to replace my large amount of blood loss was wreaking havoc.

At first, the doctors thought it might be a seizure or possible stroke. The hospital staff rapidly whisked me off to be x-rayed, prodded, and scanned. Thankfully, I was heavily sedated during the multiple moves and manipulations.

As I came out of the drug-induced sedation I was *not* expecting to see my oncologist sitting in the chair across from my bed. It didn't make any sense. I was in the hospital for shoulder surgery. In my fog, I reasoned maybe he was just stopping by to say *hi* as he made his evening rounds.

He was talking to me, but what he exactly said didn't register.

He kept apologizing and telling me how sorry he was. I asked him several times to repeat what he said, trying to wrap my mind around the truth of the matter.

Ironically, several of my doctors were at an event when the results of my scan came through. Each of their cell pagers went off at the same time with the same message. My oncologist volunteered to be the one to come to the hospital to talk with me about the pager message. He jokingly told me he had drawn the short straw.

Cancer. Again.

The MRI scan earlier in the day revealed I had a brain tumor at the base of my skull in the parietal-occipital region. Due to the size and location of the tumor—he had to refer me to an oncology team about an hour away. He laid out several options several physicians on *Team Tuk* talked about.

At the time, the physicians weren't sure *what* the tumor was—if it was metastases from one of my cancers, a *meningioma* that had taken up residence in the left occipital region of my brain, *or...* some other kind of tumor. Whatever the case, it had grown quickly, aggressively and was about the size of a golf ball and needed to be dealt with.

I felt like I was in a time warp and it was ten years earlier, reading the introduction to *Loose Screws and Skinned Knees*. Bill and I sat in the oncologist's office on that frigid January 2010 morning. An angry Arctic wind howled through the vents and open spaces in the room. With tears in his eyes, the oncologist apologized and then asked the question, "So... how are we going to do this?"

My attention returned to the present as my brain registered those very same words.

"So... how are we going to do this?"

"The only way we know how," I replied. "Straight on, head held high... taking it one day at a time."

We were grateful for the advances in medicine over the last decade, especially living in Alaska. We not only had new members on the team, but the two hospitals in Alaska were networked with The Mayo Clinic and the University of Washington. That partnership meant the hospital in Anchorage had the same cutting edge technology, networking and equipment available to them as Mayo and the UW. It also meant I didn't have to travel to the Lower forty-eight for treatment.

Bill and I were given three options: wait and watch (no one thought that advisable), radiation, or surgery with possible radiation follow-up. We decided to consult with three other oncologists who specialized in brain tumors and a neurosurgeon, also known for his expertise in complex cases before making our final treatment choice.

The radiation oncologist teamed up with a neurosurgeon, who, according to the other doctors I sought opinions from, are two of the younger super-stars in the local area and state brain surgery arena. "Nothing but the best for the best for *MY Lady*," my husband said as he hugged me tightly, squeezing any fear out of me.

The decision was made. Because of the size, the fact the tumor was aggressive, and so the tumor could be biopsied to know "what" it was, I had brain tumor surgery. At least it was something new and different! I now have more screws than before the shoulder surgery, plus I have added several more holes to my head.

I said to the team, "Good Lord, don't I have enough screws and holes in my head? I definitely already have enough rocks from being in my quarry!

No comments from the peanut gallery, please.

As I recuperated from brain surgery, sporting a new tattoo that goes from the top of my head to the nape of my neck, taking it one day at a time, hitting life straight on, head held high I speak like Yoda™ more than I speak normal English, and I have visual cuts and loss that may be permanent. Dear people are helping me to get this into your hands. I have a peace that passes all understanding with this latest adventure, even though I don't understand all the whys and wherefores.

Life has shown me time and again that what God says is true. Tomorrow *will* have enough cares and battles of their own. Whether the battle is a scourge of a worldwide pandemic like Covid-19, or when a recent routine CT revealed a solitary plasmacytoma of my sixth rib, (tumor) with no viable treatment options (due to the tumor's location), God is with me.

I am living proof prayer works. God's Will *will* be done as He numbers my days and He promises me He is in *all* the details… even on the days I think I *must* be related to Job.

The numerous front line medical combat missions and battles I've fought over the years have taken their toll. Battling cancer, recovering from multiple surgeries and subsequent rehabilitation, can be draining not only physically, but emotionally, financially and spiritually as well. "Matthew 6-ing it" is the way I keep things in check.

Verses twenty-five through twenty-seven tell us this:

"*Therefore I tell you, do not worry about your life, what you will eat or drink; or about your body, what you will wear. Is not life more than food, and the body more than clothes? Look at the birds of the air; they do not sow or reap or store away in barns, and yet your heavenly Father feeds them. Are you not much more valuable than they? Can any one of you by worrying add a single hour to your life?*" NIV

Then we go to verses thirty-three and thirty-four:

"*But seek first his kingdom and his righteousness, and all these things will be given to you as well. Therefore do not worry about tomorrow, for tomorrow will worry about itself. Each day has enough trouble of its own.*" (NIV)

As we go through each new day as it dawns, I pray you will lean on these verses and wise words. As we learn to live with the nuances of each new day, may you find the comfort and peace God *will* give you, as you seek Him, and take life one day at a time.

62

ONE LAST STORY

All of us have days, weeks, and seasons where it seems easier to wimp out. But what does that really solve? It usually only leaves more work to climb up the hill we've slid down, or uncover the mess we have let accumulate.

When I want to wimp out, I go back to a talk I gave several years ago at a *Guns and Roses - Alaskan Girlfriends Group* event.

This group did many things together. One month they might have a tea party or take in an off-Broadway production. The next month might find them at the gun range for target practice. Many women in Alaska conceal and carry; not just for personal safety, but for hunting with their hubbies and family members, but more importantly they carry when they go hiking. They never know when they might run into a moose or a bear!

Anyway, back to the event. *Guns and Roses* were putting on what was called "O Frontier! What Shall I Wear?" It included an Alaskan Fashion Show, a dessert social, and two speakers—of which I was one.

The evening started with a slideshow of vintage, pioneer Alaska, while the women enjoyed talking and partaking of decadent desserts.

After dessert, the first speaker spoke on the "Pioneer Spirit" regaling the history of one of the very first woman to come to Alaska, arriving in Skagway. The speaker was all decked out, dressed in period clothing. You talk about *not* being a wimp!

The woman highlighted—Harriet Pullen—arrived with little money. Being creative, she set to work doing what she knew best: baking pies and doing laundry. Soon the gold rush men made her one of the wealthiest women—in real estate and finances in all of Alaska.

Amazed by the bravery of dear Harriet, I was tickled to know a fashion show came next before I spoke. And it was not just any fashion show mind you. *All* of the outfits were made from duct tape! (Did you know the Walmart in Wasilla, Alaska sells more duct tape than any other store in the world? Fun Fact.)

The women's fashion parade started with pioneer-period dresses of the late 1800's, then progressed on to farming attire—including "union-suit" long johns! The models delighted the crowd as they displayed the finery of the 1920's flapper dresses, twirling their duct-taped beaded necklaces. The women's' creativity was nothing short of astounding as the runway became filled with wardrobes representing every decade up to modern-day attire, including prom dresses. It was *amazing*!

Then, it was my turn. My speaking topic was to be about "New Frontiers." I had struggled for weeks on what I was going to say. It came down to the very last day before a light bulb went on in my head and would know a bit of what I would share.

The week of the event, we had been experiencing winds of sixty to one-hundred miles an hour. (Not that any of you in the Lower forty-eight hear about our yearly over 70 mph plus wind weather.) *Everyone* was anxious for the Big Blow to be over. Power outages, downed trees, and gusts blowing over even the heartiest! I was anxious not only over the wind and the event, but Bill was working out in a remote village in the Bush of Alaska. I had been on my own for a week. As I was watching the wind drop to a mere forty to fifty mile an hour winds on our digital weather station, I suddenly heard a loud *BANG*!

Good heavens! My husband's propane gas BBQ grill had blown over. *Seriously*? The BBQ had been secured before my husband left. It had endured winds up to 100 miles an hour. And *now* it gets pushed over with a slight forty mile an hour gust? Good grief! With none of the neighbors available to help me get the BBQ upright, I decided to let it stay on its side. After all, my medical lifting limit was only five to seven pounds. My decision held until I started to smell gas. "Great," I sighed to myself. "Now what should I do?" My options were less than slim.

As the seconds ticked by, I realized there was only one thing to do. Somehow, I had to heave it upright by myself, as the propane tank was leaking. Did I mention it was also twenty degrees below zero outside?

I pulled on my thermal bib overalls, pulled up my heavy boot socks, and jammed my feet into my camouflaged boots, with cleats attached. Next I pulled on my neoprene face mask (this weather could produce frostbite faster than you can blink), wrapped my hiking scarf around my neck, and pulled my Arctic snow hat on. The last items I had to put on were my heavy-duty, winter coat and work gloves. I felt like the Abominable Snowwoman by the time I was done.

I made my way out to the BBQ, first fighting with the storm screen door refusing to stay closed. Each time I got close to making sure it was latched, a gust blasted me backward. Finally, I made it over to the downed disaster. This was a job for Mr. Incredible, *not* me, much less solo. I prayed, "Lord, help me not to hurt myself, and *puhleeze* protect the house from this leak."

Shortly after I'd huffed out my prayer, the light bulb went off in my head.

"So, *that's* what I'll speak about tonight regarding New Frontiers. Thanks, Lord!" I spoke into the wind, praying my words rode on the wind to Heaven, reaching the One who has never failed me.

I huffed and I puffed, and I hefted the heavy BBQ back into its upright position. Another miracle, as I *am* a physical wimp nowadays! I secured the BBQ to the best of my ability and leaned into the gusty headwinds to battle the storm door again. Once inside, I boot-jacked off my knee high boots and cleats, unbundled myself from the layers of clothes, and headed to warm myself by the woodstove. As I thawed myself out, I began to formulate the words for the evening's event.

My thoughts sorted out and a plan made, I took a quick shower, and then headed off to the event. The event was also going to be a book signing event for my first book, *Loose Screws and Skinned Knees*. I arrived early to set up the book table and quickly gave instructions to my helpers. Time was tight between setting up, getting last minute details in order, speaking and at the end of the event, the book signing.

I was dressed in my favorite Native Alaskan Kuspik. The fabric pattern was eagle feathers. The colors are steel blue and gray. It was made by an Aleutian elder, who told me the kuspik she had made for me was worn for traditional ceremonial events.

I often wear the beautiful garment when I am speaking or at book signings.

The evening for the *Guns and Roses* event began and I sat at a back table enjoying the company of several women I knew. Toward the end of the fashion show, I excused myself and slipped out a back door. I went out to my SUV. I grabbed my winter gear and speaking items I had bundled up earlier in the day, after hefting up the BBQ. I also grabbed two arrows.

As I made my way back to the church, I stumbled and broke one of the arrows—an older wooden arrow—in half. I wasn't sure what I was going to do... until I went into the ladies room to get dressed. One of the models for the fashion show was hurriedly duct taping the last part of her outfit. Of course! I could duct tape my arrow together and it fit into the story—and the evening—perfectly. I thanked the young lady as she hurriedly left the ladies room, then I followed close behind.

Instead of heading to where I had been instructed to enter—where the models went onto the stage—I snuck over to another room where there was a door leading into the sanctuary. I heard the applause and peeked out to the curtain call and encore parade of the duct-taped Frontier models. My heart was in my mouth.

"*This is for You, Lord. I don't have any notes, so whatever I'm going to say, it's all You.*" My prayer shot heavenward.

I heard the MC, who happened to be a First American, Inuit Native of Alaska, call my name. She called it again. I watched through a slit in the door with glee. Women's heads turned this way and that, looking for me.

"I know I saw Care!" the MC spoke into the microphone. "I know she's here. She's wearing a ceremonial kuspik!"

From the back corner of the room I emerged. With cleats on my boots and my ski pole trekking stick in hand. I wandered around the tables and looked Heavenward, and loudly spoke, "Lord? After forty years of battling everything thrown at me, is *this* Heaven? Nahhhh, it can't be… I don't see any angels around here. I *know* these ladies!"

Laughter filled the room.

I wandered over to the table where the senior pastor's wife had a look of horror as I walked on the carpet with my cleats.

"Don't worry about my cleats ruining the carpet," I told her. "It's the exact same carpet we have in our house. I know how to walk on it without snagging it."

The pastor's wife blushed and smiled.

I made my way to the stage. I hadn't anticipated how hot it

was going to be, standing under the spotlights–especially with my kuspik, and all my layers of outside gear. I turned to the cute young, Native MC and said, "You're a mom of five, can you help me get out of my snowsuit?" I used the stage stairs as a boot jack, to pull off my cleated boots, then pulled my Birkenstocks® from their hiding place under the worship piano and slipped them on. With my neurological balance deficits, it actually was (unintentionally) comical. But that is not the *real* story.

I started with, "I'm not sure I can top the portrayal of Harriet Pullen, the first woman in Skagway. Somehow, your fearless leaders think I might have something to say about heading into New Frontiers. I hate to disappoint you, but I don't have *any*thing. Zip. Nada."

(Lonnnng pause.) The ladies looked at each other with various quizzical looks.

"But God does!"

"God asked me to share with you, as you leave tonight, remember you will be heading out into New Frontiers—each and every day. And, God wants you to know one of his traits is being the Master Archer.

"As Master Archer, He holds each one of us in His quiver. Yes, I know that's pretty scary, all being lumped together. Some of you ladies are like a Nordstrom type arrow—all frilly and decked out. Some of you are an REI type with your hiking and outdoor apparel."

I pointed to some of the younger women. "I bet you are a Gap, Old Navy, or Forever 21 type arrow. Am I right?"

They nodded their heads.

"Me? With all my bionics, loose screws, and skinned knees? I'm a Walmart special. You know, duct-taped together." I pull out my broken and haphazardly taped arrow from my kuspik pocket and the women around the room start laughing.

I continued. "We are lumped all together. Just like tonight. Mingling, sharing, and enjoying each other's company. We are all in God's quiver. And in His quiver, where are we? We are on His back being carried. We are close to His heart. In His quiver, we are given a time of waiting, a time of learning, a time of resting. When the Master Archer pulls us from the quiver, He knows *exactly* where he wants us to go. He knows our assignment."

The women were intent on listening at this point. Some had frowns on their faces, others had trepidation. A few held smiles.

"God gently picks us out of His quiver. He places us in the bow, pulling us tight. He pulls us tighter and tighter until we think we will break. But where are we, really? We are in His Hands and we are the closest to His heart as we can be. When He is ready and has His sight set on where He wants to send us, He lets us go.

"Some of us—people like my husband—hit the target dead center. Bull's-eye! Many of us hit the target or maybe a little off center, but still on target. Then there are people/arrows like me: all bolted and screwed up, duct-taped together and totally miss the target and end up in a cow pie. Go figure."

More laughter.

I looked up to the ceiling. "*Oops*! Sorry, Lord. I missed the mark... *again*."

"I imagine Him lovingly chuckling and saying, 'Are you going to just sit there and wallow in the mess of manure? You know if you stay there long enough, you'll get burned, don't you? A cow pie is just manure. And manure is fertilizer. Sit in too much fertilizer, and you can get burned. Just like a plant can get burned with too much fertilizer."

Several of the audience members nodded. They'd seen it first-hand at some point.

So I dared to go on. "You see, we have to remember He is the

Vine, and we are the branches, made to bear fruit. Too much fertilizer won't produce much fruit, will it?"

As the ladies in the audience responded, I took a deep breath and continued.

"I felt the Presence of the One walk over to me—the broken, duct-taped, missed-the-mark arrow—and He reached out to pick me up, wiped me off, and went to put me back in His quiver. I argued with Him. 'What are you doing? I *stink*! You can't put me back into the quiver with all those Nordstrom or REI types. Even the Target types will be ashamed of me."

"But I felt as if God gently replied, "The others are not *your* problem. That's *My* job. I will deal with the others. *Don't take on a battle that is not yours to take on.* Besides, they could *all* use a little fertilizer. I consider it "Miracle Grow" and I assure you, mine is better than the store-bought kind.

"Once I put you back in the quiver, keep in mind it is a season of rest for you. It is a time for respite and renewal. Take the time to grow from your exposure to the fertilizer. Enjoy this rest time for you as you rub off onto others, as they will rub off on you—no matter the fragrance you each emit. It won't be long, and you will be ready to be used for My glory."

Nods and words of affirmation filled the room.

"So my friends, the next time you want to wimp out, the next time you totally miss the target, the next time you end up in a cow pie, whisper the words "Miracle Grow….it's just Miracle Grow," and you *will* rub off on others, no matter what!

"My final words to you are: Blessings and s'mores – and remember: *Don't Wimp Out!*"

RESOURCES

Joni and Friends™

For the past 40 years, *Joni and Friends™* mission has been to present the hope of the Gospel to people affected by disability through programs and outreaches around the world. The organization energizes the church, and moves people from lack of awareness to embracing people of all abilities into the fabric of worship, fellowship, and outreach. Joni and Friends™ also train and mentor people with disabilities to exercise their gifts of leadership and service in their churches and communities.

www.joniandfriends.org

Wm. Paul Young

William Paul Young, also known as Wm. Paul Young or simply, Paul Young, is a Canadian author. He wrote the novels *The Shack*, *Cross Roads*, and *Eve*, as well as a theological book – *Lies We Believe About God*. He is well known for his various videos, international speaking events and influential Christian leadership.

www.wmpaulyoung.com

Don Woodward

Don is a graphic designer, photographer and creative director for *Ideawave* in Portland, Oregon. He participates in spiritual life with *The Open Table Conference*, *The Gathering Fire* and *Imago Dei Community*. He also is a member of a folk-rock band named *John Nilsen & Swimfish*.

www.ideawave.com

Jenne Rogers, PhD.

Co-author of *Summer Surprises/ Brave: Be Ready* and *Victory is Easy.*

www.summertimepress.com

David Naster – You Just Have To Laugh (YJHTL)

David Naster is a director and actor, author and comedian, known for *You Just Have to Laugh*, *Terminal Interface* (2003) and *Star Search* (1983). Find him on *YouTube*.
www.naster.com

Dr. Linda Hawes Clever, MD, MACP

Linda is a member of the *Institute of Medicine of the National Academy of Sciences*, Clinical Professor of Medicine at *UCSF*, Associate Dean for Alumni Affairs at the *Stanford University School of Medicine*, founding Chair of the Department of Occupational Health at *California Pacific Medical Center*, and former Editor of the *Western Journal of Medicine*. She is also founding President of *RENEW*, a not-for-profit aimed at helping devoted people maintain (and regain) their enthusiasm, effectiveness and purpose, and author of *The Fatigue Prescription, Four Steps to Renewing Your Energy, Health and Life*.
www.thefatigueprescription.com

Mary Beth Carlson Music

Mary Beth createg a consistent flow throughout her recordings with an elegant, beautifully distinctive style that became a best-selling "signature sound" throughout the country. Mary Beth passionately played from the heart, whether it was romantic pop standards, inspirational arrangements, or original compositions inspired by people who touched her life. Each piano orchestral album features an hour or more of music to relax refresh and inspire; uniquely beautiful treasures you will want to experience and share over and over again. When I write, it is usually with her music playing in the background.
www.marybethcarlson.com

Christen Morrow Ara   Young Life - SW Capernaum Ministry Director

Christen has 20+ years of ministry experience with youth with disabilities in California and Latin America. She serves with Young Life, overseeing Capernaum (disability ministry), for 5 states. Christen and her husband, Christian, live in Central California with four children.
www.younglife.org

Kimberley Woodhouse

Kim is a devoted wife and mother, and a third generation Liszt student. She has passed down her love of music and the arts to hundreds of students over the years, recorded three albums, and appeared at over 2,000 venues. Her quick wit, enthusiasm, and positive outlook through difficult circumstances have gained her audiences at conferences, retreats, churches, military functions, and seminars all over the country.

The Woodhouse family's story has been on the front page of newspapers, in magazines, articles, medical journals, and most famously featured on ABC's Extreme Makeover: Home Edition. They were also asked to share their story on The Montel Williams Show and Discovery Health Channel's Mystery ER along with hundreds of other TV appearances and radio interviews. She is an award-winning, best-selling, prolific author who can be reached at:

www.kimberleywoodhouse.com

Tracie Peterson

Tracie Peterson is an author of Christian fiction. She writes many historical novels, with romantic threads in them, as well as writing with other Christian authors on joint novels. Many of her books are published by **Bethany House**. She originally used the pen name of Janelle Jamison.

www.traciepetersonbooks.com

John Klapperich – Klapperich and Associates, LLC

JKlapperich & Associates believes that any situation can be tailored to enhance your life and help you achieve your goals. They believe people who are successful in this world are the people who get up and look for the opportunities they need, and if they can't find them, they make them.

www.jklapperich.com   *mrjnk@hotmail.com*

Electra Ariail – My Gratitude Buddy

My Gratitude Buddy is a tool to help you live your BEST life. You can use it to snap into presence, check-in with yourself or be reminded of your awesomeness. Email Electra at if you need a little help uncovering it. When you load My Gratitude Buddy up with a list of short messages/prompts to yourself that make you reflect, feel good, or help get you back into flow, and My Gratitude Buddy will randomly send you those messages throughout the day.

www.mygratitudebuddy.com

Bill and Tim Tuk – WISPhotography

Don't call him a photographer. Don't call him an artist. Just call him Bill. Bill Tuk is a lifelong native of Alaska. It only took him 45 years to move to the state his heart has always called home. Bill says of his pictures, "God put me in the right place at the right moment with my camera in hand" These prints are NOT edited. What the camera (and Bill) saw, is exactly what you get to see, supreme examples of Alaska's beauty found off the beaten path or just outside his front door. The pictures speak for themselves, so, enjoy!

www.wisphotography.com

ABOUT THE AUTHOR

Care Tuk is an internationally known speaker, educator, and retreat/workshop leader. She was a school and rural home health occupational therapist before retiring and writing *Loose Screws and Skinned Knees*. She was named Top 5 Business Woman in America by *Wyndham Resorts*, *American Airlines*, and *Liz Claiborne* (2001), recognizing her work with youth, disability outreach, and awareness. She continues being a tireless health advocate, encouraging others to live a full life despite a life full of battles and hidden disabilities.

Care lives at the base of the Talkeetna Mountains in Alaska.

Visit her website at – www.caretuk.com